FOUR OFFALY SAINTS

Four Offaly Saints

THE LIVES OF

*Ciarán of Clonmacnoise, Ciarán of Seir,
Colmán of Lynally*
AND
Fíonán of Kinnitty

PÁDRAIG Ó RIAIN

FOUR COURTS PRESS

Typeset in 11.5 pt on 14 pt Garamond by
Carrigboy Typesetting Services for
FOUR COURTS PRESS LTD
7 Malpas Street, Dublin 8, Ireland
www.fourcourtspress.ie
and in North America for
FOUR COURTS PRESS
c/o ISBS, 920 NE 58th Avenue, Suite 300, Portland, OR 97213.

A catalogue record for this title is available
from the British Library.

ISBN 978–1–84682–704–4

SPECIAL ACKNOWLEDGMENT

The author and publisher would like to acknowledge the
support of the Heritage Office, Offaly County Council.

Printed in England
by TJ International, Padstow, Cornwall.

For Méabh, Íde and Max

Contents

Illustrations

COLOUR PLATES
(*between p. 46 and p. 47*)

Abbreviations

AClon.	*Annals of Clonmacnoise being the Annals of Ireland from the earliest period to A.D. 1408*, ed. D. Murphy (Dublin, 1896)
ACoC	*The antiquities of County Clare: John O'Donovan, Eugene Curry*, ed. M. Comber (Ennis, 1997)
AConn.	*Annála Connacht: The Annals of Connacht (AD 1224–1544)*, ed. A.M. Freeman (Dublin, 1944)
AFM	*Annála ríoghachta Éireann: Annals of the kingdom of Ireland by the Four Masters*, 7 vols, ed. J. O'Donovan (Dublin, 1848–51; 2nd ed. 1856; facs. repr. with introduction and appendix by K.N. Nicholls, Dublin, 1990)
AI	*The Annals of Inisfallen (MS Rawlinson B.503)*, ed. S. Mac Airt (Dublin, 1951)
AICO	*Archaeological inventory of County Offaly*, ed. C. O'Brien & P.D. Sweetman (Dublin, 1997)
Anecd.	*Anecdota from Irish manuscripts*, 5 vols, ed. O.J. Bergin et al. (Halle & Dublin, 1907–19)
ATig.	'The Annals of Tigernach', ed. W. Stokes, in *Revue Celtique* 16 (1895), 374–419; 17 (1896), 6–33, 119–263, 337–420; 18 (1897), 9–59, 150–97, 267–303; repr. 2 vols (Felinfach, 1993)
ATig. Index	*The Annals of Tigernach: index of names*, D. Ó Murchadha, Irish Texts Society, Subsidiary Series 6 (London, 1997)
AU	*The Annals of Ulster (to AD 1131)*, ed. S. Mac Airt & G. Mac Niocaill (Dublin, 1983)
b.	barony
bb.	baronies
Br	Brussels, Bibliothèque Royale MS 2324–40
CGSH	*Corpus genealogiarum sanctorum Hiberniae*, ed. P. Ó Riain (Dublin, 1985)
Co.	County
CS	*Chronicum Scotorum. A chronicle of Irish affairs from the earliest times to A.D. 1135*, ed. W.M. Hennessy (Rolls Series, London, 1866)
DIL	*Dictionary of the Irish language, based mainly on old and middle Irish materials*, ed. E.G. Quin et al. (Dublin, 1913–76, compact ed. 1983)

DIS	*A dictionary of Irish saints*, P. Ó Riain (Dublin, 2011)
facs.	Facsimile
gen.	genitive
GRSH	*Genealogiae regum et sanctorum Hiberniae* (Maynooth & Dublin, 1918).
HDGP	*Historical dictionary of Gaelic placenames: Foclóir stairiúil áitainmneacha na Gaeilge*, i, ii, iii, iv, v, vi, ed. P. Ó Riain, D. Ó Murchadha, K. Murray & E. NicCarthaigh (Irish Texts Society, London, 2003, 2005, 2008, 2011, 2013, 2016)
IrT	*Irish Texts* i–v, ed. J. Fraser, P. Grosjean & J.G. O'Keefe (London, 1931–4)
LisL	*Lives of the saints from the Book of Lismore*, ed. W. Stokes (Oxford, 1890)
ll.	lines
Lr	Lower
M	Marsh's Library, Dublin, MS Z.3.1.5
MartD	*The martyrology of Donegal: a calendar of the saints of Ireland*, ed. J.H. Todd & W. Reeves (Dublin, 1864)
MartG	*Félire hÚi Gormáin: The martyrology of Gorman*, ed. W. Stokes, Henry Bradshaw Society 9 (London, 1895)
MartO	*Féilire Oengusso Céli Dé: The martyrology of Oengus the Culdee*, ed. W. Stokes, Henry Bradshaw Society 29 (London, 1905; repr. Dublin, 1984)
MartT	*The martyrology of Tallaght*, ed. R.I. Best & H.J. Lawlor, Henry Bradshaw Society 68 (London, 1931)
MS	manuscript
MT	Version of text in M and T manuscripts
N.	North(ern)
nr	near
ODCC	F.L. Cross & E.A. Livingstone (eds), *The Oxford dictionary of the Christian Church* (Oxford, 1997)
OSLGY	*Ordnance Survey letters, Galway*, ed. M. Herity (Dublin, 2009)
p.	page /parish
R	Bodleian Library, Oxford, MS Rawlinson B 485
RIA	Royal Irish Academy
S	Bibliothèque Royale, Brussels, MS 7672–4 (*Salmanticensis*)
S.	South(ern)
s.a.	*sub anno*

St	Saint
Stowe	Royal Irish Academy, Dublin, MS A iv1
s.v.	*sub vocabulo*
T	Trinity College Dublin, MS E.iii.11
tn	town
Upr	Upper
v.l.	varia lectio
W.	West(ern)

COUNTIES

AH	Armagh	LH	Louth
AM	Antrim	LK	Limerick
CE	Clare	LM	Leitrim
CK	Cork	LS	Laois
CN	Cavan	MH	Meath
CW	Carlow	MN	Monaghan
DB	Dublin	MO	Mayo
DL	Donegal	OY	Offaly
DN	Down	RN	Roscommon
DY	Derry	SO	Sligo
FH	Fermanagh	TE	Tyrone
GY	Galway	TY	Tipperary
KE	Kildare	WD	Waterford
KK	Kilkenny	WH	Westmeath
KY	Kerry	WW	Wicklow
LD	Longford	WX	Wexford

Preface

FOLLOWING THE PUBLICATION OF *Four Tipperary saints* in 2014, Amanda Pedlow, Heritage Officer of Offaly County Council, invited me to prepare a similar volume on the saints of Co. Offaly.[1] Coincidentally, four Offaly saints also became subjects of Lives, and this allowed me to adopt much the same format for this volume as for my previous publication. It may of course be argued that a fifth Offaly saint, Mochuda of Rahan, also became the subject of a Life but, as I pointed out in *A dictionary of Irish saints*, the Life written for this saint shows signs of having been compiled at his later foundation at Lismore in Co. Waterford.[2] The Latin Lives of the two saints named Ciarán have previously been translated into English. In 1921, R.A.S. Macalister published a translation of all Latin and Irish Lives written for Ciarán of Clonmacnoise, and Ingrid Sperber published a translation of the Life of Ciarán of Seirkieran in 1998.[3] The notes added to both previous translations have proved especially useful.

The encouragement received from Amanda Pedlow and other regular attendees at the Roscrea conferences organized by George Cunningham has been a great help in the preparation of this volume. Offaly County Council generously allocated funds towards the costs of the publication, and supplied, through its Heritage Office, some of the illustrations that accompany the book. I am indebted to all authors of the images and especially to Roger Stalley.

I am grateful to my wife Dagmar for encouragement and advice, and to our son Diarmuid for his assistance in solving some cruxes. The book is dedicated to my three youngest grandchildren. Finally, I have to thank Four Courts Press for agreeing to publish the volume, the Press's reader for some helpful suggestions, and Martin Fanning in particular for the care he took in seeing it through the press.

---

1 Ó Riain, *Four Tipperary saints.* 2 *DIS* 471. The vernacular text concerning Mochuda's expulsion from Rahan, which has been edited and translated by Charles Plummer (*Bethada*, i, 300–11), although compiled in the Rahan area, does not qualify for description as a saint's Life. 3 Macalister, *Latin and Irish Lives*; Sperber, 'The Life of St Ciarán'.

Introduction

LIVES OF SAINTS

IF HAGIOGRAPHY IS NOT HISTORY, as is now generally held, what value attaches to Lives of saints? Largely confined to patrons of substantial churches, Irish saints' Lives can be of considerable value, not because they throw much light on their subjects but because they reveal how the traditions surrounding the saints might be used to protect and promote the interests of the communities that held them in high regard. Typically, Lives were compiled against a background of change, which explains why their production was markedly periodic. After four Lives had been compiled in the period 650 to 700 – two of Patrick, one each of Brighid and Colum Cille – there was a long interval until the first half of the ninth century, when one Latin (Brighid) and two vernacular Lives (Brighid and Patrick) were produced. The following three hundred years saw the production of very few Lives, almost exclusively by writers from the ecclesiastical communities of Armagh, Kildare and Kells (which had taken over the leadership of the Columban community from Iona). The disruptive period that followed the beginning of the English conquest of Ireland in 1169 was one of intense hagiographical activity, and the bulk of the surviving record of the Irish saints, liturgical and literary, dates to this period. In my view, the four Offaly Lives covered by this volume also belong in the period after the arrival of the English.

MARTYROLOGIES AND CALENDARS

The record of the feastdays of the Irish saints was also periodic in character. About 830, an abbreviated Northumbrian version of the continental Hieronymian martyrology – previously used in the churches of Iona and Bangor – was considerably enlarged at the monastery of Tallaght, mainly by reference to patrons and founders of churches associated with the so-called *céili Dé*, an eremitical group within the Irish church. The Tallaght martyrology, which survives in a twelfth-century manuscript, was also given metrical form by its compiler, a bishop named Óengus (Aonghas). Both prose and metrical

versions record the feasts of the Offaly saints featured in this volume, and
Colmán of Lynally is accorded the rare privilege of having the prose text record
the day of his birth as well as the day of his death. Equally rare was the manner
in which the September feast of Ciarán of Clonmacnoise found its way into
the mid-ninth-century martyrology compiled by a monk named Usuard at
Saint-Germain-des-Prés in Paris. In addition to the feasts of Ireland's three
national saints, Usuard noted those of Ciarán, Cainneach of Aghaboe and
Fiontan of Clonenagh, presumably on the basis of information received from
a Midlands informant. Usuard's text later became the main component of the
Roman Martyrology, which is used wherever Roman Catholic liturgy is
practised, and which still records the feasts of the three Midlands saints. The
feasts of Ciarán of Clonmacnoise and Colmán of Lynally were also recorded
in a calendar, possibly compiled in Glendalough, which was brought by an
Irish pilgrim to the monastery of Reichenau on Lake Constance in Germany.
In the late twelfth century, several new martyrologies, based in part on the
ninth-century Tallaght martyrologies, were produced in churches associated
with the canons regular of St Augustine. In all of these, the feasts of the four
Offaly saints were again recorded.

DATES OF MANUSCRIPTS

With the notable exception of the early Latin Lives of Patrick, Brighid and
Colum Cille, the surviving copies of saints' Lives, including those in this
volume, are found almost exclusively in manuscripts dating to the fourteenth
or fifteenth century. Brighid's ninth-century vernacular Life, for example,
which is arguably the earliest surviving saint's Life written largely in Irish,
survives in a manuscript copied shortly before 1500. The same manuscript
contains a copy of the ninth-century vernacular Life of Patrick, and the version
of this text chosen by its modern editor is only twenty years older, dating to
1477. In both cases, the copies of the Lives were written for lay patrons,
unconcerned with the preservation of the tattered and blackened exemplars
used by their scribes. Similarly, the manuscript that contains the earliest
surviving copies of the Lives of the Offaly saints featured in this volume, the
so-called *Salmanticensis* manuscript, now in the Bibliothèque Royale in Brussels,
dates, at the earliest, to the early fourteenth century.

SAINTS' GENEALOGIES

According to a seventeenth-century account, the no longer extant early eleventh-century *Saltair* of Cashel contained pedigrees of the saints, but the earliest manuscript versions that survive – the Book of Glendalough (*c.*1130) and the Book of Leinster (*c.*1160–70) – date to the twelfth century. Two of the four Offaly saints in this volume figure in both twelfth-century manuscripts, but Ciarán of Clonmacnoise and Fíonán of Kinnitty are only in the Book of Leinster. As the saints were thought to have lived in the remote past, hagiographers and genealogists were prone to reshape their histories, and pedigrees proved particularly susceptible to localization and manipulation. Apart from Fíonán of Kinnitty, whose descent is consistently attached to the Corca Dhuibhne of west Kerry, the genealogy of each of the saints featured here shows signs of manipulation. However, despite their unreliability as genuine statements of origin, saints' pedigrees can be useful indicators, both of the spread of cults and of the local interests to which they regularly fell prey. For this reason, they are fully deserving of the respect shown to them by modern scholars.

TERRITORIAL DIVISIONS

The territorial division into counties, which underlies the present study, is a relatively modern creation, first introduced to Ireland by the English administration in the sixteenth century, when what is now known as Offaly was designated King's County. After Ireland attained its independence in 1921 the name Offaly began to be used, somewhat inaccurately, since the Uí Fhailghe, who gave name to the county, controlled only the lands lying east of the town of Tullamore (baronies of Geashill, Lower and Upper Philipstown, Coolestown and Warrenstown), together with the present baronies of East and West Offaly in Co. Kildare. The lands west of the town of Tullamore consisted of a patchwork of ancient kingdoms, comprising Fir Cheall (baronies of Eglish, Ballycowan and Ballyboy), Éile (baronies of Clonlisk and Ballybritt), Dealbhna Bheathra (barony of Garrycastle), and the southern edge of Teathbha (barony of Kilcoursey). None of the churches featured in the present volume lay in ancient Uí Fhailghe: Clonmacnoise was located in Dealbhna Bheathra; Seirkieran and Kinnitty in Éile, and Lynally in Fir Cheall.

Lying just south of the line that divided Ireland's two halves, Leath Chuinn to the north and Leath Mhogha to the south, the churches of the present county of Offaly could scarcely have been other than intermediaries between the two. A vision attributed to Finnian of Clonard saw a silver moon rise above Clonmacnoise that brought brightness and light to the mid-parts of Ireland, and another vision attributed to Ciarán himself showed the shadow of his church protecting every part of the country, north and south. While no such vision is attributed to Colmán of Lynally, he is not only said to have come from the North, his church demonstrably maintained close relations with northern churches until at least the eleventh century. Similarly, although Fíonán's main church was at Kinitty, his Life deals mainly with his activities in south-west Kerry, where there were numerous dedications to him in the Killarney and Waterville areas. Connections such as these bear witness to the important role played by the churches of Offaly in the history of early Irish Christianity.

Editorial policy

THE TRANSLATION OF THE TEXTS, though faithful, is not literal. Its purpose is to provide readable and easily comprehensible texts. Consequently, such usages in the Latin texts as the recurrent application of *sanctus*, 'holy', to the saint's name are often ignored here, as are the repetitive naming practices which are again characteristic of the Latin texts. Connectives (and, but, when, while, where etc.) are often either added or omitted, and demonstatives (this, that) are often replaced by the articles (a, the). Sometimes, when they add nothing to the sense of the words about them, such terms as 'however' (Latin *autem*) are also omitted. As a rule, placenames are rendered here by their anglicized forms but, where these are either unknown or no longer used, the Irish forms are retained. Similarly, territorial names are anglicized where appropriate, as in Ossory for Osraighe, but left unchanged where confusion might occur, as in Midhe, which denoted mainly Westmeath; Múscraighe Tíre, which denoted what are now the baronies of Ormond; and Éile, which comprised baronies in both Tipperary and Offaly. Personal names are given their classical Irish forms.

As none of the Lives can be discussed in isolation from the church associated with its subject, an account of the relevant church's documentary history, in as far as this can now be established, will be given in the introduction to each translation. To avoid clutter in the translations, notes to the texts are added at the end of the volume. Finally, with a view to facilitating use of the volume, lists of abbreviations, sources, and an index have been provided.

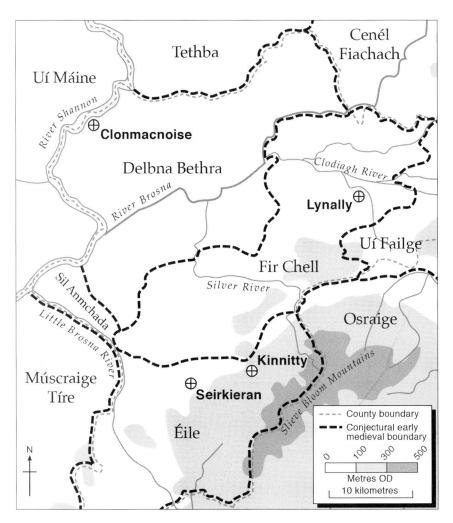

1. Map showing locations of the principal churches of the saints featured in this volume. Original map by Caimin O'Brien, taken from *Stories from a sacred landscape* (2006), modified here by Matthew Stout.

The Life of Ciarán of Clonmacnoise

THE SAINT

A LTHOUGH MOST VERSIONS OF THE saint's genealogy provide Ciarán with an Ulster background, the separate lines of descent traced for him sometimes vary considerably. The earliest version, preserved in the twelfth-century Book of Leinster, attaches him through his father Beoaidh (also written Beodhán, Baodán and Beonaidh) to the descendants of the Ulster hero, Fearghas son of Róch.[1] In doing so, however, it lists names which are equally at home among the Conmhaicne of the barony of Carra in Co. Mayo – where there is a dedication to Ciarán in the parish of Ballyovey – and among the Corca Mruadh, who gave name to Corcomroe in Co. Clare.[2] For its part, the vernacular version of the saint's Life agrees with a lone version of the corpus of saints' pedigrees, by providing Ciarán with an altogether different descent from Eacha son of Muireadh, a legendary ancestor of the Ulstermen.[3] Descent from Eacha, who gave name to Lough Neagh (Loch nEachach), established for the saint a genealogical association with such other saints as Colmán Eala of Lynally, Seanán of Laraghbryan and Maol Ruain of Tallaght.[4] To complicate matters further, a note added to the Book of Leinster pedigree attaches Ciarán to the 'seventh group' of the Latharna Molt, who gave name to the town of Larne in Co. Antrim.[5] The opening chapter of his Latin Life provides yet another twist to the story of the saint's ancestry; it places the people of Latharna in the region of Midhe, now mainly county Westmeath.

The saint's father, described as a *saor*, 'craftsman or carpenter' – whence the common designation of the saint as *Mac an tSaoir*, 'Son of the Carpenter' – is said to have spent some time in captivity in Wales before escaping back to Ireland. There he made his way to Ceinéal Conaill, a name used for what

1 *CGSH* §125.1.   2 Included in the pedigree are Cas son of Fraoch son of Cúscraidh, ancestor of the Conmhaicne of Carra in Co. Mayo, and Modhraoi, eponymous ancestor of the Corca Mruadh of Corcomroe in Co. Clare. Ciarán of Seirkieran was venerated in south-east Clare, but the dedication of a well in the parish of Killofin, barony of Clonderalaw, formerly east Corca Bhaiscinn, may well have been to Ciarán of Clonmacnoise (*ACoC* 144). Ciarán and Seanán, patron of Corca Bhaiscinn, are brought together in the Life (§22).   3 *LisL* ll. 3975–81; *MartO* 204.   4 *GRSH* 95–7.   5 The kingdom of Midhe, though mainly the county of Westmeath, also extended into the neighbouring county of Offaly,

2. Inscribed stone at Fuerty church, Co. Roscommon, drawn by George Petrie and
first published in M. Stokes (ed.), *Christian inscriptions in the Irish language*
(Dublin, 1878), plate viii.

is now approximately the territory covered by the diocese of Raphoe.[6] From
there he is said to have moved on to a place called 'Ráith Chriomhthainn' on
the plain between Roscommon town and Elphin where, according to local
tradition, his son Ciarán was born in the parish of Fuerty.[7]

Sometimes taken to have been Patrick's sister, the saint's mother Dairearca
is otherwise traced through a father named Earcán to a branch of the Ciarraighe
of north-east Kerry (Iorluachair), who also traced their remote descent to
Fearghas son of Róch.[8] She is said to have met Ciarán's father in a territory
called 'Ceinéal Fiachrach', probably a slightly corrupt form of Ceinéal Fiachach
(later 'Kenaliagh') in the Westmeath barony of Moycashel.[9] There the saint

where Clonmacnoise was situated. Cf. Ryan, *Clonmacnois*, 26–7.   6 *CGSH* §125.2. Why Ceinéal Conaill
was chosen is unclear. I know of no dedication to Ciarán in the diocese.   7 According to his early Lives,
Patrick founded the church of Fuerty and left there Deacon Ius(tus) who went on 'in old age' to baptize
Ciarán out of a book Patrick left in the church (Bieler, *Patrician texts*, 146 §28(2). Cf. Stokes, *Tripartite
Life*, 104; Mulchrone, *Bethu Phátraic*, ll. 1176–82). Ciarán's Life gives Iustus an alternative name Diarmuid
(§1).   8 *CGSH* §§125.2; 722.16.57; *LisL* ll. 3983–90.   9 *HDGP* iv, 123–5.

is remembered at Templemacateer (Teampall Mhic an tSaoir) in the parish of Ardnurcher where, it has been suggested, the burial place of Ciarán's father, brother and three sisters was located.[10] Ciarán is described by the genealogists as the third child of eight, but little else is recorded of his siblings beyond their names, place of burial, and the attachment of two brothers to a church named Íseal Ciaráin, apparently near Clonmacnoise (§22).[11] Before her liaison with Ciarán's father, Dairearca reputedly gave birth to a son named Mac Arda by a man called Fiodhach of the Ciarraighe Luachra, the ruling family of north Kerry. A tract styled 'The West Munster Synod' describes Mac Arda, who was later to become king of Ciarraighe Luachra, as Ciarán's uterine brother.[12] This would establish a relationship between Ciarán and Fíonán of Kinnitty, who is said by the genealogists to have been a son of Maonach son of Mac Arda or, if we follow the evidence of Fíonán's own Life (§2), of Mac Arda (Airdhe) himself.

Ciarán came to be regarded as one of Ireland's apostles, a distinction he shared with his namesake Ciarán of Seirkieran, together with some other pupils of Finnian of Clonard.[13] Moreover, he is said to have resembled in manners John the Apostle, Christ's 'beloved disciple'.[14] Unusually for an Irish saint, he is thought to have died young; his age at death, which occurred, according to the annals, in 549, within a year of the foundation of Clonmacnoise, is put variously at thirty-one, thirty-four and, Christ-like, at thirty-three.[15] His feast, which represents the day on which he is thought to have died, is assigned by almost all martyrologies and calendars of saints to 9 September.[16] Writing about 830, Aonghas of Tallaght, Ireland's earliest known martyrologist, did not hold back in his praise of Ciarán. The quatrain he devoted to the saint at 9 September reads in translation:[17]

> Great the festival that filleth countries,
> that shaketh swift ships … ,
> of the wright's son beyond kings,
> the fair feast of Ciarán of Cluain.

10 Walsh, *Placenames*, 255; Kehnel, *Clonmacnois*, 314 §58 (on the plausible assumption that *Teach Mhic an tSaoir*, which is mentioned in the saint's vernacular Life (*LisL* ll. 3999–4000), was identical with *Teampall Mhic an tSaoir*). 11 For a discussion of the identification of Íseal Ciaráin with a site in the parish of Ballyloughloe, see Swift, 'Sculptors and their customers', 115–16. 12 Meyer, 'Laud genealogies', 315. 13 Heist, *Vitae*, 83 §5. 14 *CGSH* §712.6. 15 *ATig s.a.*; *AU s.a.*; §31 below. Máire Herbert ('An infancy narrative') draws attention to many other features of the saint's Life that underline his likeness to Christ. Included among them is his status as son of a carpenter. 16 *MartT* 69, 96; *MartO* 193; *MartG* 172; *MartD* 240–2. 17 *MartO 193*. The translation is by Whitley Stokes. The original Irish text reads:

The assertion that the festival 'filleth countries' turned out to be prophetic; a little over thirty years later, Ciarán's feast was recorded in a martyrology compiled by the Benedictine monk Usuard at Saint-Germain in Paris. While noticing the days of Brighid and Patrick – by then established feasts in continental sources – Usuard added at 9 June the feast of the third-most important Irish saint, Colum Cille. Furthermore, perhaps due to the presence of an Irish monk of Midlands origin at Saint-Germain, he added the feasts of Ciarán of Clonmacnoise, Fiontan of Clonenagh and Cainneach of Aghaboe.[18] Usuard's martyrology went on to become the most popular of all medieval documents of its kind, and Baronius adopted it as the main source of the Roman Martyrology he compiled in 1583–4, which has since been used wherever the Roman rite is practised. Ciarán's feast has thus remained part of the universal Roman commemorative record from the ninth century down to the present day, even though very few non-Irish Christians would have been familiar with the history of the saint or known the precise location of his church. The feast also found its way into a copy of the Hieronymian martyrology kept on the Reichenau in Lake Constance in southern Germany, where an early ninth-century calendar of Irish origin also noted it.[19] Although not quite as widespread, dedications to the saint are numerous, and not only in Ireland, where they are mainly found in Connacht and the western part of Leinster, the parts of the country most influenced by Clonmacnoise.[20] Perhaps because of Colum Cille's reputedly high regard for him, Ciarán was also widely venerated in Scotland.[21]

    Many relics were associated with the saint and venerated accordingly at Clonmacnoise and elsewhere.[22] One, a gapped bell known as *Bearnán Ciaráin*, was rung on occasion to register the community's disapproval of the actions of lay rulers. Other relics included Ciarán's altar, his crozier, called *Óireanach*, 'gold-faced', and what may have been his gospel-book, called *Matha Mór*, 'great Matthew'?[23] These relics were used occasionally to protect secular rulers, as in the case of an Ua Maoil Sheachlainn king of Midhe who, despite their

Mór líth línass crícha, crothass longa lúatha, Maicc in tshaír tar ríga, féil chain Chiaráin Chlúana.
18 Dubois, *Martyrologe d'Usuard*, 300; *In Scothia, Quaerani abbatis.* As Jaques Dubois (ibid., 101) suggested, Usuard is likely to have been told of these feasts by an Irish informant, presumably a native of the Midlands.   **19** Schneiders, 'The Irish calendar', 58: *Ciarani meic ind Sair*; *Acta sanctorum Novembris* II, 497–8: *sancti Kerani confessoris.*   **20** Kehnel, *Clonmacnois*, 242; O'Hanlon, *Lives*, ix, 236–7.   **21** The Scottish dedications are listed in Forbes, *Kalendars*, 436; Watson, *The history of the Celtic placenames*, 278. Cf. O'Hanlon, *Lives*, ix, 235.   **22** Ó Floinn, 'Clonmacnoise: art and patronage', 93–6.   **23** *AFM* s.a. 1143; *AClon* 197. Local tradition knew Ciarán as 'Kieran of St Matthew' (*Christian Examiner*, 822) and §16 of his Life claims that he read this gospel while with Finnian in Clonard.

SEPTEMBRIS 9. 503

& Didio paffus eft tempore D.octetiani, de quibus Eufeb.li.8.c. 25. & Niceph.li. 7.c.16. Diuerf s hos effe inter fe, tùm diuerfitas temporum, tum fociorû oftêdit.

d Timothei & Faufti.] De his item Vfuardus, & alii recentiores hac die.

e Eufebij & foc.] Horum nobile certamen fcribit Sozomenus libro 5. cap. 8.

f Neftoris.] De quo etiam idem So- rom. vna cum prædictis martyribus agit vbi fupra lib. 5.c.8.

g Corbiniani epifc.] Apud Bedam de eodem hac die. Eius res geftas fcriptis mandauit Aribo Epifcopus Fifingen. quas habet Surr. tom. 5. Plura de eodem Otho Frifing.lib.5.cap. 23. & 24. Claruit temporibus Gregorij Secundi Papæ circa annum Domini 730.

9 Quinto Idus Septemb. Luna. G xv

a	b	c	d	e	f	g	h	i	K	l	m	n	p	q	r	f
17	18	19	20	21	22	23	24	25	26	27	28	29	30	1	2	3
t	u	A	B	C	D	E	f	F	G	H	M	N	P			
4	5	6	7	8	9	10	11	11	12	13	14	15	16			

Icomediæ paffio SS.mart. Dorothei, & Gorgonij, qui apud Diocletianum Auguftum honores ampliffimos confecuti; cum perfecutionem, quam ille Chriftianis inferebat, deteftarentur, præfente eo, iuffi funt primo appendi, & flagris toto corpore laniari, deinde vifceribus pelle nudatis, aceto & fale perfundi, ficq; in craticula affari, atq; ad vltimum laqueo necari. Interiecto autem tempore, B. Gorgonij corpus Romam delatum fuit, ac via Latina pofitum, & inde ad Bafilicam S. Petri translatum. In Sabinis, trigefimo ab Vrbe milliario, SS.martyrum Hyacinthi, b Alexandri, & Tiburtij. Sebaftæ S. Seueriani c militis Licinij Imp. qui cum quadraginta martyres in carcere detentos frequens vifitaret, iuffu Lyfiæ Præfidis faxo ad pedes ligato fufpenfus, ac verberibus cefus, & flagris laniatus, in tormentis reddidit fpiritum. Eodem die paffio S. Stratonis, d qui pro Chrifto ad duas arbores ligatus atque difcerptus, martyrium côfummauit. Item SS.martyrum Ruffini, & Ruffiniani fratrum. Romæ i S.Sergij Papæ, & confefforis. In territorio Taruanenfi S. Audomari g Epifcopi. In Scotia S.Querani h abbatis.

3. The feast of Ciarán of Clonmacnoise in final position in the list of entries for 9 September in Caesar Baronius's 1585 edition of the Roman Martyrology.

protection, was made captive in 1143 by Toirdhealbhach Ua Conchubhair, king of Connacht.[24] Yet another relic, known as *adhart Chiaráin*, 'Ciarán's pillow', figures in the story of how Cairbre Crom, a king of Connacht, was restored to life.[25] Furthermore, the hide of a dun cow (*Odhar Chiaráin*), allegedly brought by Ciarán to Clonard when he went to school there, is said to have given name to the famous late eleventh- or early twelfth-century *Leabhar na hUidhre*, 'Book of the Dun Cow'.[26] Relics of the saint also found their way to the Continent, among other places to Sens in north central France and, possibly, to Ferrières in the same general area, where, according to a mid-ninth-century manuscript, relics of his were kept, together with those of other Irish saints.[27]

Ciarán was not the only saint associated with Clonmacnoise; several early successors of his also came to be regarded as worthy of the honour. These included his immediate successor Aona, alias Aonghas, who died, according to the annals, in 570 and was remembered on 20 January.[28] Aona figures in the Life written for Ciarán (§25), who is said to have foretold his succession while on Hareisland in Lough Ree. Aona also figures in other Lives, such as those of Colum of Terryglass and Daigh of Inishkeen.[29] Aona's successor, Mac Nise, who was also regarded as a saint, plays a role in the vernacular version of Ciarán's Life as one of eight companions present when Clonmacnoise was founded.[30] At least six other abbots of Clonmacnoise are to be found in the Irish calendar of saints, together with two bishops, thus providing the church with an array of saints exceeded among Irish churches by Bangor and Armagh only.[31]

THE CHURCH

The prominence of the Clonmacnoise saint in the hagiographical record was no doubt largely due to the outstanding role of his church as a centre of cultural

---

24 *AFM* 1143.   **25** Meyer, 'Wunderbare Geschichten', 225.   **26** Plummer, *Vitae*, i, 205 §15; Best & Bergin, *Lebor na hUidre*, ix.   **27** Mordek, 'Von Patrick zu Bonifatius'.   **28** *DIS* 77.   **29** Heist, *Vitae*, 233, 392.   **30** *LisL* l. 4375.   **31** Ó Riain, *Feastdays*, 66–7. The entries are as follows: *Cronán*, gl. *abb Clúana meic Nóis, MartG* 138. *Aodhlugh ... abb Clúana maic Nois, MartG* 44 (= *MartD* 56). *Baítani episcopi Clúana, MartT* 20 (= *MartG* 46, v.l. *Cluana maic Nois; MartD* 60). *Cronbice ab. Clúana, MartT* 30 (= *MartG* 70, v.l. *abb Clúana mac Nóis; MartD* 96). *Lucrid*, gl. *abb Clúana meic Nóis, MartG* 86 (= *MartD* 112). *Abb Clúana in Lucell*, gl. *abb Chluana mic Nóis, MartO* 215, 220 (= *MartD* 268). *Caoncomhrac, epscop, ó Inis Endaimh ... acus rob eapscop hé i cCluain mic Nóis ar tús, MartD* 198. *Corpre Crom ... epscop Clúana maic Nóis, cenn crabuidh ermhoir Erenn ina re, MartG* 48 (= *MartD* 66).

and politico-ecclesiastical activity up to the end of the twelfth century.[32] Lying close to the boundary between Ireland's two halves, north and south, the church was founded in 548–9, according to the annals, and more precisely, if we are to believe the saint's vernacular Life, on the eighth of the calends of February, now 25 January.[33] This is otherwise the feast of the conversion of St Paul at Damascus, which may well be why the day was chosen. The church took its name from a vassal tribe named Maca Nóis, who were allegedly swineherds, a common association of ecclesiastical foundations, as is shown, for example, by the story of the foundation of Patrick's first church at Saul in Co. Down, which involved the swineherd of the local king.[34] The Book of Ballymote provides the eponymous ancestor Nós with a descent from Síghe son of Dealbhaith, ancestor of the Dealbhna, a branch of whom, Dealbhna Bheathra, ruled over the area in which Clonmacnoise is situated.[35]

Such was the church's early importance that it already found mention in two seventh-century Lives of saints. Adhamhnán's Life of Colum Cille describes how its subject, while residing in Durrow, paid a visit to Clonmacnoise, where he was given a welcome warm enough to suggest that there was then a close relationship between Ciarán's church and Iona.[36] Patrick's biographer Tíreachán was less favourably disposed towards Ciarán's church; he maintained that Clonmacnoise was forcibly holding several churches rightly belonging to Armagh.[37] Yet, the same author states that Ciarán was baptized by a disciple of Patrick named Iustus who had previously baptized the people of Uí Mhaine, a territory on the edge of which Clonmacnoise was located.[38]

Though doubtless forcible in some cases, Clonmacnoise's hold on other churches grew to be quite considerable. The extent of its possessions (and claimed possessions), amassed over the centuries, is set out in detail in a seventeenth-century English translation of the church's *Registry*. According to this, the church mainly possessed lands in the Connacht counties of Roscommon, Mayo, Sligo and Leitrim and, east of the Shannon, in the Leinster counties of Offaly and Westmeath.[39] The consequent wealth of the church would have enabled it to wield considerable power, and exercise influence over a wide area. Ciarán's Law (Irish *cáin*), a further source of revenue for the church, was promulgated over the kingdom of Connacht on a number of occasions,

---

32 Bradley, 'The monastic town'. 33 *Dormitacio filii artificis .i. Ciaraini ... postquam Cluain Mc. Nois construere cepit, AU* 549.1 (= *ATig.* 548); *LisL* l. 4374. 34 Mulchrone, *Bethu Phátraic*, ll. 376–7. 35 Atkinson, *The Book of Ballymote*, 191ac29–33; cf. *HDGP* v, 133. 36 Anderson & Anderson, *Adomnán's Life of Columba*, 214, 218. 37 Bieler, *Patrician texts*, 142 §25 (2), 146 §28 (2). 38 Ibid., 146 §28 (3). 39 Kehnel, *Clonmacnois*, 238–42; eadem, 'The lands of St Ciarán'.

in 744, 788 and 814. In fact, it continued to be invoked until well into the twelfth century, as is shown by the notice of the death in bed under its protection in 1151 of Cormac Ó hEaghra of Luighne, Co. Sligo.[40] Various kings sought and received the protection of Ciarán's relics, doubtless against payment.[41] However, wealth of this kind was just as liable to attract envy and hostility. Over the centuries, the church was subject to numerous plundering raids and burnings to which the annals bear recurrent witness. The index to the Annals of the Four Masters, for example, which has more entries on Clonmacnoise than on any other church, records no fewer than nine burnings and sixteen plunderings.[42]

The considerable attention paid by the annalists to the church's affairs extended to its various officials, abbots, bishops, vice-abbots, priors, priests, anchorites, lectors and scribes, thus providing the church with a fuller record than any other Irish church.[43] Not surprisingly, other churches sought good relations with Clonmacnoise, an example being Glendalough which appears to have succeeded in establishing with it an *aonta*, 'union of prayer and interest, covenant'.[44] The church also found favourable mention in early ninth-century *céili Dé* documents associated with the church of Tallaght. Óengus of Tallaght (*c*.830) held up its 'choirs lasting melodious' as a shining example of a flourishing Christianity and, like Armagh which immediately precedes it, Clonmacnoise retained the martyrologist's attention for the space of two full quatrains.[45]

The monastery was highly valued as a 'retirement home' for deposed royalty. The Annals of the Four Masters, at 979 (*recte* 980) and at 1134, record the death of a notable person staying at, or connected with, Clonmacnoise.[46] Similarly, Murchadh, grandson of the 'high-king' Aodh Allán († 743), having been deposed by his cousin Niall Caille in 823, retired to the monastery of Clonmacnoise, where he died, according to an Irish calendar kept on the Reichenau in southern Germany, in the tenth year of his 'pilgrimage'.[47] The church was much favoured as a place of burial.[48] We are told in the Life (§27) that 'both kings and chieftains of the Uí Néill and Connachta' are buried at Clonmacnoise with holy Ciarán. The privilege of being buried in the church's cemetery (or cemeteries) indeed seems to have been highly prized, to judge

---

40 *AU s.a.* 744, 788, 814.; *AFM s.a.* 1151.   41 *AClon s.a.* 642; *ATig. s.a.* 973, 1089.   42 *AFM Index*, 34–5.   43 Ryan, 'Abbatial succession'; idem, *Clonmacnois*, 25–58; Bhreatnach, 'Learning and literature', 97–8; MacDonald, 'The cathedral'.   44 Mac Shamhráin, 'The unity of Cóemgen and Ciarán'.   45 *MartO* 24–5 (ll. 177–84).   46 At the earlier date, the deceased was Aghdha, king of Teathbha; at the later date Céileachair, a member of a well-known scribal family connected with the monastery (MacDonald, 'The Cathedral', 132).   47 Schneiders, 'Irish calendar', 57.   48 Swift, 'Sculptors and their customers', 106–8; Bhreatnach, 'Learning and literature', 100–3.

by some surviving verse. In one couplet, the church is lauded as the burial ground of the warriors of the Northern Half of Ireland (*reilic láech Leithe Cuinn*); in another, it is said to be the resting place of many kings (*Hi ccathraigh ... Ciarán ... fil mór do ríoghaibh*).[49] The head of Diarmuid son of Cearbhall, one of the chief ancestors of the southern Uí Néill, who controlled the high-kingship over a long period, is said to have been kept in the church, and many of his descendants were buried there.[50]

A place of great distinction, as the *Triads of Ireland* claim, the monastery was famous for its stonework, high crosses, round tower – one of two only in Co. Offaly – and no less famous for the breadth of its learning.[51] The saint's Life (§25) maintains that, as Ciarán was leaving his brothers, he blessed them and, taking on his shoulders satchels with books in them, he went on his way. The image is appropriate, and the church's pursuit of learning is borne out, not only by the frequent references in the annals to its *fir léighinn* (lectors / professors), but also by the number of manuscripts once held in its library, some still extant, others known to have once been part of it.[52] Best known among the extant manuscripts is the previously mentioned vellum Book of the Dun Cow (*Leabhar na hUidhre*), which contains the earliest surviving versions of several important texts, including the Cattle-Raid of Cooley (*Táin Bó Cuailnge*).[53] Also extant are copies of sets of annals once held by the library, such as the Annals of Tigernach, *Chronicon Scotorum* and, albeit in a seventeenth-century English translation, the Annals of Clonmacnoise.[54] The previously mentioned English translation of the church's *Registry* has also survived.[55]

A final measure of the church's importance is its choice in 1111 as a diocesan see with charge of the territory of what is now mainly Westmeath, and its selection, possibly in the 1140s, as the location of a priory of canons regular.[56] The Augustinian canons often located their priories in close proximity to cathedrals, and the convent of canonesses at Clonmacnoise, known as the 'Nuns' Church', is said to have adopted, like the priory, the strict Arroasian form of the rule.[57]

---

49 Best, 'Graves of the kings', 164; O'Keeffe, 'The kings buried in Clonmacnois, §§1, 16; Ó Floinn, 'Clonmacnoise: art and patronage'.   50 *ATig. s.a.* 564.   51 *Ordan Hérenn Clúain Maic Nóis / Trí clochraid Hérenn: ... Cluain Maic Nóis*, Meyer, *Triads*, §§2, 34. *gan dul tar crosaibh Chluana*, Best, 'Leabhar Oiris', 94 §48. Fitzpatrick & O'Brien, *Medieval churches*, 22–3; Bhreatnach, 'Learning and literature'. 52 *AFM s.a.* 789, 855, 921, 948, 977, 988, 999, 1005, 1034, 1038, 1054, 1063, 1080.   53 Best & Bergin, *Lebor na hUidre*, xxxiii, 142–206; Bhreatnach, 'Learning and literature', 99–100.   54 *ATig.; AClon.* Cf. Kelleher, 'Táin and the Annals', 117.   55 Kehnel, *Clonmacnois*.   56 Gwynn & Hadcock, *Medieval religious houses*, 64–5, 165.   57 Ibid., 315.

THE LIFE

Several Lives of the saint survive in Latin and Irish.[58] The Latin text survives
in three recensions, the Irish in one only. It has been suggested that the
'primitive' or original Life was written no later than the ninth century, but
this seems far too early for a text which, to judge by the longer recension in
the Marsh's Library manuscript, is replete with associations that point to the
twelfth century at the earliest.[59] Among these is the prominence given to
Finnian of Clonard, whose church rivalled Clonmacnoise for primacy among
the churches of the kingdom of Midhe (mainly Westmeath), each becoming
both a diocesan centre and the seat of an Augustinian priory.[60] According to
his Life (§§15–18), Ciarán attended the famous school run by Finnian at
Clonard. While there, Finnian foretold that his pupil's authority would extend
over 'half of Ireland'. Ciarán is also assigned a critical role in the story of a
house of nuns at Clonard, which may reflect the founding there of St Mary's,
a house of Augustinian nuns, by Murchadh Ua Maoil Sheachlainn (†1153),
king of Meath.[61] One of Murchadh's daughters (Agnes) became abbess of St
Mary's, while another (Dearbhfhorgaill) rebuilt the Nuns' Church at
Clonmacnoise in 1167.[62] In the absence of a full investigation of the Life,
associations such as these may be viewed as indicators of a (late) twelfth-
century date.

    Since both Clonmacnoise and Clonard hosted priories and convents of
Augustinian canons and canonesses, one would expect to find many traces of
this in the saint's Life. In addition to the saint's association with Clonard, there
are at least three other episodes that point to probable Augustinian influence.
First of these is the choice of Ciarán's teacher Diarmuid, whose church on
Inchcleraun in the Longford parish of Cashel became the site of a priory of
canons.[63] Second, Hareisland (Inis Ainghin) in the Westmeath parish of
Bunown, where Ciarán spent some time, was likewise the site of a house of
canons on Lough Ree.[64] Third, Ciarán's return from the dead involved an
exchange of vestments and the establishment of a *fraternitas* with Caoimhghin
of Glendalough, where the canons also had a priory.[65]

    A lively memory of the saint and his deeds, his 'afterlife', as it were, survived
in the Clonmacnoise district well into the nineteenth century. Caesar Otway,

---

58 See Plummer, *Vitae* I, xlviii–li and Kenney, *Sources*, 378–80.   59 Kenney, *Sources*, 379.   60 For
Clonard, see Gwynn & Hadcock, *Medieval religious houses*, 63–4, 163–4.   61 Ibid., 314.   62 *AFM s.a.*
Cf. Ní Ghrádaigh, 'But what exactly did she give', 175–80.   63 Gwynn & Hadcock, *Medieval religious
houses*, 178.   64 Ibid., 177.   65 Ibid., 176–7. Cf. Mac Shamhráin, 'The unity of Cóemgen and Ciarán'.

> Darby Claffy, as not having
> received his shilling, was still in attendance. "Can
> you tell me any thing, Darby, about the beginning of
> these buildings, and about the consecration of the
> place." "By course, I can, sir," said he; "I recol-
> lect, at any rate, what all the people before me have
> *said* about it:—Kieran, the carpenter's son, came
> directed by God's finger, to this place, which was then
> called Drum Tipraid, or, as one would say in English,
> the brow of the hill that is in the centre of the land.
> It was a green sheep-walk in those days, and belonged
> to Dermot O'Melaghlin, king of Meath. 'Give me,
> says the saint to the king, 'a spot of ground where I
> may build a house in honour of God, and enclose a
> place where the dead may receive Christhen berrin.'
> 'I cannot afford to give my best land for that purpose,'
> said the churlish king.

4. Extract from [Caesar Otway], *A tour in Connacht comprising sketches of Clonmacnoise, Joyce Country, and Achill* (Dublin, 1839), p. 111.

who visited Clonmacnoise in the early 1830s on the day after the celebration of Ciarán's feast of 9 September, met a local named Darby Claffy, who regaled him with memories of Ciarán, some of which echoed episodes in the Life of the saint.[66] Claffy identified 'Drum Tibraid' as the place at which Ciarán founded his church, a name recorded as *Tibraid* in the saint's Latin Life (§28), *Ard Tiprat* in the vernacular Life and *Druim Tibrat* in other references to Clonmacnoise.[67] Claffy also recounted how Ciarán performed a miracle that persuaded the owner 'Dermot O'Melaghlin' to grant him the site. Intended is Diarmuid mac Cearbhaill, remote ancestor of the Ua Maoil Sheachlainn kings of Midhe, who, according to the tale of Diarmuid's death, was with Ciarán when he began to build his church.[68] Finally, Claffy went on to identify an image on the Cross of the Scriptures as Ciarán holding in his hand the gospel of St Matthew, a book which figures prominently in the Life's account of the saint's term at school in Clonard (§17).

66 Otway, 'A day at Clonmacnoise'; idem, *A tour in Connacht*, 67–116.   67 Stokes, *Lives of the saints*, ll. 4371–2; O'Grady, *Silva Gadelica*, 72; Hyde, 'The adventures of Léithin', 133.   68 O'Grady, *Silva Gadelica*, 72–3.

The version of the saint's Life translated here is from Marsh's Library, Dublin, manuscript Z. 3.1.5 (formerly V.3.4). Among the typical features of this version is the compiler's interest in topography, illustrated here by numerous indications of exact location of churches. Cases in point, among others, are Clonard (§15), Scattery Island (§22), Clonmacnoise (§28) and Seirkieran (§30).

MANUSCRIPTS AND PREVIOUS EDITIONS

The Life survives in three Latin and two vernacular versions. The Latin recensions are Marsh's Library, Dublin, Z.3.1.5 (formerly V.3.4), f. 144[d] ff.; Bodleian Library, Oxford, Rawlinson B 485, f. 91[b] ff. (copied in Rawlinson B 505, f. 127[b] ff.); Bibliothéque Royale, Brussels, 7672–4 (*Codex Salmanticensis*), 77c. The Latin text of the Marsh's Library manuscript has been edited in Plummer, *Vitae*, i, 200–16, and previously translated in Macalister, *Latin and Irish Lives*, 15–43; the Brussels text has been twice edited, by De Smedt and De Backer, *Acta*, cols 155–60, and by Heist, *Vitae*, 78–81.

The vernacular Lives survive in two manuscripts, the Book of Lismore, ff. 35[b]–39[d] and Bibliothéque Royale, Brussels, manuscript 4190–200, 154[a]–170[b]. The Lismore text has been edited and translated by Stokes, *Lismore Lives*, 117–34, 262–80, and again translated by Macalister, *Latin and Irish Lives*, 66–97. The Brussels text has yet to be edited.

The present translation is based on the Marsh's Library manuscript.

The Life of Ciarán of Clonmacnoise

THE LIFE OF ST CIARÁN, ABBOT OF CLONMACNOISE

Here begins the Life of St Ciarán, abbot and confessor

1 ~ Holy abbot Ciarán belonged to the people of Latharna in the region of Midhe in the middle of Ireland. His father, called Beoaidh,* a rich carpenter, took a wife named Dairearca who bore him five sons and three daughters. The sons, of whom four became priests and one a deacon, were born in this order, and named as follows: first, Luiceann; second, Donnán; third, holy abbot Ciarán; fourth, Odhrán; fifth, Crónán the deacon. Of the three daughters, named Luighbheag, Raichbhe and Pata, the two first were holy virgins whereas the third, Pata, was first married and afterwards a holy widow. When the carpenter Beoaidh became greatly weighed down by taxes imposed by Ainmhire, king of Tara, he avoided their imposition by moving out of the bounds of Midhe into the lands of Connacht and settling in the plain of Aoi, near Criomhthann the king. It was here that Ciarán, the subject of this Life, was born. His birth was foretold by the druid of the aforesaid king, who said in front of all: 'The son in the womb of Beoaidh's wife will be held in honour before God and men and, as the sun shines in the sky, so too will he shine in Ireland through his holiness'. Holy Ciarán was afterwards born in the fort called Ráith Chriomhthainn, in the plain of Aoi in the province of Connacht. He was baptized by a holy deacon called Diarmuid in Irish but later named Iustus. It was only appropriate that a just man be baptized by a man named Iustus. Holy Ciarán was reared in that place by his parents and God's grace appeared in him through all things.

2 ~ One day, the best horse of the aforesaid king Criomhthann's son Aonghas died suddenly, and the boy was greatly saddened at this. When he had fallen asleep, still saddened, a shining figure of a man appeared to him in his sleep, saying: 'Do not be sad concerning your horse, for there is among you a little boy, Ciarán son of the carpenter Beoaidh, who can revive your horse through

---

* The Latin text has the form Beonnadus. See note to the text at p. 90.

God's grace. Let him pour water, while praying, into the horse's mouth and onto its face, and it will rise up healthy, and let you offer the child a gift on account of your horse brought back to life'. Awakened from his sleep, Aonghas, the king's son, told his friends about these words, before coming to Ciarán and bringing him to where the horse lay dead. When the pious youth Ciarán poured water onto its mouth and face, the horse rose from the dead and stood strong in front of all. At that, the king's son made a grant to Ciarán in perpetuity of the place, which was both very good and large.

3 ~   On another day, Ciarán's mother reproached him, saying: 'Other sensible boys bring honey daily to their parents from fields and places where honey flows, but our son, guileless and meek, brings none to us'. Hearing these words of his mother, the holy boy hurriedly went to a nearby well and filled from it a vessel of water, which, when blessed and made into the very best honey, he gave to his mother. Marvelling at this miracle, his parents took the honey to Iustus the deacon, Ciarán's baptismal father, so that he might witness the miracle wrought through God by the boy whom he baptized. When he had heard and seen this, Iustus gave thanks to Christ and prayed for the boy.

4 ~   While minding the cattle of his parents, the boy Ciarán read the psalms with Diarmuid, but the teaching was done in a way for us most miraculous. Ciarán tended the flocks in the southern part of the plain of Aoi while Diarmuid lived in its northern part, so that a large tract of land lay between them. They greeted one another from a distance, with gentle words across the space of the plain. The old man taught the boy from his church across the plain and the boy read while seated on a rock in the open country. This rock, which now has the cross of Christ on it, is called by the name of Ciarán, and is still venerated today. Through divine will, the saints heard one another, while others did not hear them.

5 ~   On a certain day, when Ciarán was minding the cattle, a cow gave birth to a calf in his presence. At that hour, on seeing a miserable, thin and hungry wolf approaching, the pious boy said to him: 'Go miserable one and eat the calf', which it did, devouring it. When the holy shepherd arrived home with his cattle, the cow, searching for its calf, cried out loudly. When she saw this, Ciarán's mother Dairearca said to him: 'Where is that cow's calf? Give it back, whether from land or sea, for you have lost it and its mother's heart is greatly distressed'. When Ciarán heard these words, he returned to where the calf had been devoured and collected its bones into his lap; then, coming

back, he placed them in front of the wailing cow. Immediately, through divine compassion and because of the boy's holiness, the calf rose up in front of all and stood soundly on its feet, playing with its mother. Then a clamour in praise of God arose from those present, who blessed the boy.

6 ~ As the pious Ciarán was going out to a certain homestead nearby, cruel and malicious laymen set a very fierce dog on him, to devour him. When he saw the fierce dog approaching him, Ciarán quickly thought of the psalmist's verse, and said: 'Lord, deliver not up to beasts the soul that trusts in thee'.[†] As the dog ran on strongly, through divine will its head entered a calf's ring, and now caught in the ring it struck its bound head against the tree from which the ring was suspended until the head broke. When they saw this, they were greatly afraid.

7 ~ At another time, when some thieves came from another territory, they found Ciarán alone, reading beside his cattle. They thought of killing him and stealing the cattle but, while approaching him with this in mind, they were struck by blindness and could move neither hand nor foot until they did penance and appealed to him for their sight. When the holy shepherd saw them changed from their ill nature, he prayed for them and immediately their sight was restored. Returning, they gave thanks and told this to many.

8 ~ On a certain day, some poor man came to Ciarán, asking for a cow. Ciarán then appealed to his mother to give the poor man a cow, but his mother had no mind to listen to him. When he saw this, Ciarán took the poor man outside with him and the cattle, and gave him there a good cow and its calf. However, the calf was between two cows, both of which loved it. Knowing that the cow would be of no service without the calf, he gave both animals with their calf to the poor man. On the following day, in place of these, others gave him four cows in alms, which he gave to his mother who was reproaching him. He then admonished his mother in reasoned fashion, and from then onwards she was in awe of him.

9 ~ On another day, Ciarán gave the knife of his uncle Beoán as a gift to a needy man, for which he similarly received four knives on another day. Four smiths came namely from a place called Clooncrim, and gave Ciarán four knives in alms, which the holy boy returned to his uncle for the one knife.

† Psalm 73:19.

10 ~ On another day, Ciarán gave his uncle's ox to a man who begged for it. His uncle then said to him: 'Son, how shall I be able to plough today, when you have given my ox to another'. The holy boy replied: 'Put your horse under the plough with the oxen today and tomorrow you will have enough oxen'. Once placed under the yoke with the oxen instead of the ox given away, the horse immediately became tame and ploughed properly all day, just like an ox. On the following day, four oxen were given in alms to Ciarán, who handed them over to his uncle in place of his ox. When they heard of the great wonders done by Ciarán, people sought his prayers and offered him gifts.

11 ~ One day, Ciarán's father brought a small royal vessel from the home of king Furbhaidhe, to have it for some days. The king liked that vessel greatly but Ciarán, when asked by some poor people for alms in Christ's name, and not having anything, handed the king's vessel to them. When he heard this, the king became very angry and ordered that Ciarán be a captive in his service. For this reason, Ciarán was led into captivity as a servant of king Furbhaidhe and assigned work on the basis of its severity, namely the daily turning of a millstone in order to make flour. Miraculously, Ciarán sat reading next to the millstone while it swiftly turned without the hand of any man and ground out flour in the presence of all. For God's angels, whom people could not see, were grinding on Ciarán's behalf. Not long after, a man named Iarnán of the race of the Déise, who was prompted by divine will, came from Munster with two wonderful vessels similar to the king's in type and in usefulness and gave them in alms to Ciarán. When the king heard of the miracle of the millstone, he accepted those two vessels and gave his freedom to Ciarán, where before, through anger, he was not willing to accept a ransom for him. Now freed in that way from the servitude of the king, Ciarán blessed the man through whom he had found his freedom, as well as his race.

12 ~ One day when Ciarán was in a place called Cluain Innsythe, he saw a boat positioned on the river and a kiln on the riverbank. Within the kiln there was a wheel constructed from twigs and full of ears of corn, with a fire underneath to dry them for threshing, according to the western manner of Britain and Ireland. Ciarán then said prophetically and discreetly to his companions that the boat on the water would burn that day and the kiln on dry land would be under water. As they were marvelling at this and contradicting it, he said to them: 'Wait a little and you'll see it with your own eyes'. At that, the little boat was raised up from the water on to land and

placed in the kiln so that its cracks and breaks might be caulked. When the heap of wood was set on fire, the kiln and boat in the middle of it burned. Then, strong men, tearing the kiln out of the ground, threw it from the bank into the river, as the servant of the Lord had prophesied. When they heard and saw such a prophecy concerning opposite things, they gave glory to Christ who grants such a gift to his servants.

13 ~ On another day when Ciarán had come from the fields to his home, some men came towards him. He asked them where they had come from, and they said that they had come from the home of Beoaidh the carpenter. 'Did you not find appropriate refreshment there for the sake of Christ?' said he. They replied: 'No; the woman there we found to be harsh; she did not even give us a drink by way of hospitality'. When Ciarán heard this, he blessed them, before going quickly to his own home, where, on entering, he found no one, because the people were busy at work outside. Then, holy Ciarán, moved with zeal for God, scattered all the food he found in his parents' home, pouring milk on to the ground, mixing butter with sheep manure, and throwing bread to the dogs, so that no one could use it. In this way he showed it to be only proper that food not given to guests in Christ's name was to be destroyed by men, lest food of that kind be eaten. After a short while, his mother came and, on seeing the house so out of shape, she wanted to cry, greatly wondering as to what had happened to it. When Ciarán provided the reason, she calmed down and promised to change, and many of those who heard became charitable.

14 ~ Another day, with Ciarán seated in his father's cart in the middle of the countryside, the axle broke in two, which saddened the saint's father and his companions. Ciarán then blessed the axle and it straightway came together again, as it had previously been. After that, they went about successfully in the cart all day long.

15 ~ After this, Ciarán wished to leave his parents and go to the school of Finnian, a learned man, great in all forms of sanctity, in order to read the scriptures there together with all the other holy men of Ireland. He asked of his parents that a cow be led by him to the school, so as to have its milk for sustenance, but his mother refused, saying: 'Others in that school do not have cows'. Then, having received permission and a blessing from his parents – although against the wishes of his mother who wanted to keep him with her forever – he went

on his way. Reaching his parents' cattle, he blessed a cow and ordered it to follow him in the name of God. Immediately, the cow followed him with its recently born calf and, wherever he went, the cow ambled behind him as far as Clonard on Leinster's border with Uí Néill, with the monastic town itself lying within Uí Néill. When he arrived there, Ciarán made a barrier in the field with his staff, between the cow and its calf, and no way did they dare to cross it. However, though unable to cross, the cow used to lick its calf across the track of the staff and, at the appropriate hours, they used to come with a full supply of milk to their stall. As that cow was dun-coloured, it used to be called *Odhar Chiaráin* (Ciarán's dun cow), the fame of which still remains in Ireland, and so unbelievably plentiful was its milk at that time that it used to be divided among the scholars and was sufficient for many. Its hide remains today with honour in Ciarán's monastic town and miracles are wrought through it by God's grace. This is the greatest of all its virtues, as elderly holy men, disciples of Ciarán, have told us: it has been shown that, by divine influence, every man who dies while lying on it will possess eternal life with Christ. Many of the holy men of Ireland were in the school of the most holy master Finnian, namely two saints Ciarán, two saints Bréanainn and Colum, as well as many more. On his day, each of them used to grind on the quern with his own hands, but angels of God used to grind on Ciarán's behalf, as they did for him during his captivity.

16 ~ The daughter of the king of Tara was brought to Finnian so that she might read the psalms and scriptures with God's holy man, and promise a vow of virginity. As she willingly promised to keep her virginity for Christ, Finnian said to Ciarán: 'Son, let this virgin and handmaiden of Christ, the daughter of an earthly king, learn in the meanwhile with you until a church for virgins be built for her'. Since Ciarán obediently agreed to do this task, the virgin read the psalms and other lessons with him. When Finnian had placed that virgin and others in a cell, the blessed monks questioned Ciarán as to her conduct and character. Ciarán said to them: 'Truly, I know nothing of the probity of either her conduct or her body, because God knows that I never saw either her face or any other part of her, except the lower part of her clothes when she came from her parents. Nor did I exchange any words with her, except only for her readings'. The virgin, who used to eat and sleep with a certain holy widow, gave the same testimony of Ciarán, and many were strengthened in the true religion through their separate witness.

17 ~ Ciarán read Matthew's gospel with father Finnian, along with others. When he had come to the middle of the book, where it is said: 'Whatsoever you would that people should do unto you, do you likewise unto them', Ciarán said to Finnian: 'This half of the book which I read is enough for me to carry out in practice, and this single sentence is enough of teaching for me'. Then, one at the school said to all: 'From now on it is proper that Ciarán be called *Leath Matha* (Half of Matthew), but Finnian said to him: 'No, the appropriate name for him is *Leath Éireann* (Half of Ireland), for his parish will be spread over half of Ireland'. This prophecy caused much jealousy towards Ciarán.

18 ~ Another day, when Ciarán was alone in his cell, he came to table to eat food and, wishing to partake after the blessing, he said: 'Bless you'. Noticing that no one responded with 'Lord', he rose from the table without eating anything. He did the same thing on the following day, rising from the table without eating. On the third day, having fasted for three days, he came to table and said 'Bless you'. At that, a voice from heaven said to him: 'Let the Lord bless you, weary Ciarán, your prayer is now serious, for it suffices for a man when alone to bless his food in the name of Almighty God and then eat it'. In this way, Ciarán, while giving thanks, ate bread on the third day.

19 ~ On a certain occasion, he went to a king of Tara – called Tuathal Maolgharbh, because he was rough – with a view to liberating a female unjustly kept in servitude by the king, but he would not release her. Ciarán then blessed her and ordered her to go with him to her own people. Straightway rising up, she walked away from the king's house among crowds of people, without anyone seeing her until she arrived safely among her friends. At that, the king and others marvelled greatly at God's miracles.

20 ~ Another time, Ciarán went into the territory of some Connacht chieftain so that he might similarly request from him a woman unjustly held in servitude. As Ciarán was sitting there, he beheld three men coming to him with three gifts as alms; one gave him a cow, the other a mantle, the third a frying pan. Holy Ciarán gave all three to importunate poor people in the presence of the chieftain. At the very same time, he received in the presence of the chieftain larger gifts from others, namely a cooking pot with three measures for the frying pan, twelve mantles for the one mantle and twelve cows for the single cow, all of which he sent to other holy men living locally. Seeing all these

things, the chieftain generously granted freedom to the woman who, rejoicing and giving thanks, went off to her own people.

21 ~ After this, Ciarán went to the island of Aran, which is in the ocean to the west, some distance beyond Ireland. The island, in which a large number of holy men remain, has always drawn its inhabitants out of Ireland, and innumerable are the holy men lying buried there whose names are known to God only. Ciarán lived there for many a day in demanding service under the most holy abbot Éanna, and many miracles were revealed through him there, and his holy deeds are still spoken about. While there, Ciarán witnessed this wonderful vision, which was also seen by Éanna: namely a large, fruit-bearing tree on the bank of the river Shannon in the middle of Ireland, whose shadow protected every part of the country, with branches reaching into the sea beyond. On the following day, Ciarán spoke of this vision to Éanna who straightway interpreted it, while saying: 'The fruit-bearing tree you and I saw is yourself, my son, since you will be great in the presence of God and men. Your distinction will fill Ireland and the shadow of your supporting piety and grace will protect it from demons, plagues and dangers, and the fruit of your labour will assist many far and wide. By God's injunction, therefore, go quickly to the place where your resurrection will be. God will show it to you, and there you will be of help to many.' Ciarán was there consecrated a priest and thereafter, by order of Éanna, and with the prayers and blessings of all the holy men on the island of Aran, Ciarán came to Ireland.

22 ~ On a certain day, as Ciarán was on a journey, he met a poor man on the way who asked him for alms, and he gave him his hooded cloak, and went about afterwards in an undergarment only. He turned aside on his journey to Scattery Island (Inis Cathaigh) which lies in Limerick's estuary, at the entrance to the ocean, towards the setting sun, between the lands of the Ciarraighe and Corca Bhaiscinn. The most holy elder Seanán, who was the first to live on that island, was there, but a venomous and greatly harmful beast had been in sole possession of it since ancient times. By God's miracle, Seanán banished it to a certain distant lake, and a famous and holy monastic town is now on the island in honour of the saint. As Ciarán was approaching the island, Seanán foresaw in his mind the arrival of the saint and also his nakedness. He sent a vessel out to bring Ciarán to the island and, taking a cloak discreetly in his hand, Seanán went out to meet him at the harbour. When he saw Ciarán coming to him in an undergarment only, most blessed Seanán enquired

jocularly of him: 'Is it not shameful for a priest to go about in an undergarment only, with no hood'? Smiling, Ciarán replied: 'My nakedness will soon be rectified, for a cloak for me is underneath the clothes of my elder Seanán'. Ciarán stayed for some days with Seanán, deliberating on the divine mysteries, and they established between them an alliance and fraternity. Afterwards, Ciarán went on his way with a kiss of peace.

23 ~ When he left Seanán, Ciarán went to his brothers, Luiceann and Odhrán, who lived in a church called Íseal, meaning 'lowest place'. Ciarán lived with them for a time and his brothers appointed him as almoner and guestmaster. Being older, Luiceann was the abbot of that place and Odhrán the prior. Once, as holy Ciarán was reading outside in a field facing the sun, he suddenly noticed weary guests entering the hospice and, rising up quickly, he forgot his open book, which remained outside until the following day. While he was looking after the guests, washing their feet and diligently ministering to them, night soon fell. That night there was great rain, but by God's will the open book was found bone-dry, untouched by even a drop of rain, while all the ground about it was wet. Because of this, Ciarán and his brothers gave voice to the praises of Christ.

24 ~ Near that place of Ciarán was a certain island in a lake in which a chieftain and his attendants lived in their fortification, and their noise and tumult used to disturb the prayers of the holy men. When Ciarán saw this, he went out to the edge of the lake and prayed to the Lord that he give them some bit of relief from that island. On the following night, both island and lake moved through divine power to another place further away, where the noise of the crowd did not reach as far as the holy men of God. The earlier location of the lake is still visible today, partly sandy and partly wet, as a sign of the miracle.

25 ~ On a certain day, when Ciarán was working outside in a field, a poor person came to him, asking for alms. At that hour, a cart and two horses were presented to Ciarán by a certain chieftain, namely Criomhthann's son, which he handed on to the poor person. At that, since Ciarán's brothers could no longer keep up with the magnitude of his charity, for he was dividing their property daily among the poor, they said to him: 'Brother, go away from us; your generosity is so great that we cannot be with you in one place, and continue to look after and nourish our brethren'. Ciarán responded: 'If I were to stay in this place, it would not be *íseal* (low), not small but high, that is to

say great and honoured'. Having said this, Ciarán blessed his brothers and, taking on his shoulders satchels with books in them, he went on his way. Leaving the place behind a little, he found waiting for him on the road a very tame deer, on which he placed his satchels and, wherever the deer went, Ciarán followed. On reaching Lough Ree in east Connacht, the deer stopped opposite Hareisland, which is in the lake. Realizing that the Lord had called him to that island, Ciarán sent the deer away with a blessing and, entering the island, he dwelt there. Now when the fame of his holiness was heard, good men came to him from far and wide, and Ciarán made monks of them. Many alms of different kinds were also given to him by the faithful. However, a certain priest by the name of Daniel, to whom the island belonged, when prompted by devilish envy, began to expel by force Ciarán and his companions. Wishing to do good to his persecutor, Ciarán sent faithful messengers to him with a gift of kings, given to him in alms, namely a very ornate gold ring. On seeing it, the priest first refused to accept it but, afterwards, when persuaded by dutiful men, he accepted it gratefully. Full of God's grace, Daniel the priest then came to Hareisland, which belonged to him, and granted it to Ciarán in perpetuity.

26 ~ On another day on Hareisland, when he heard the voice of a man at the harbour, who wished to enter the island, Ciarán said to his brethren: 'Go, my brethren, and bring here the man who is to be your next abbot after me. Quickly sailing, the brethren found only a lay adolescent at the harbour and, having no regard for him, left him there. Returning, they said to Ciarán: 'We found no one at the harbour but a secular boy who was wandering in the woods as a fugitive. The rusticity of the person calling from the harbour is a long way from abbotship'. Ciarán then said to them to sail without delay and bring the boy quickly because, through God's revelation, he had recognized from the voice that this would be their abbot after himself. When the brethren heard this, they brought him there; Ciarán gave him the tonsure and read diligently with him. The boy was filled with the grace of God day after day, so that he became the holy abbot after most blessed Ciarán. His name is blessed Aonghas of the Laoighse.

27 ~ Ciarán's gospel-book, which some brother held carelessly in a boat, fell into the lake and remained underwater for a long time, without being found. One day, during summer time, so great was the heat that cows went into the lake to cool in the water. When they emerged from the water, the binding of the

leather satchel, in which the gospel-book had been placed, was clinging to the foot of a cow, which carried it in that way on to land. The gospel-book was found to be bone-dry and white, without any moisture, in the rotted leather satchel, as if it had been stored in a book-press. Holy Ciarán and his companions rejoiced at this.

28 ~ After this, a certain Munsterman of the Corca Bhaiscinn, Donnán by name, came to Ciarán, who was staying on Hareisland. Ciarán asked of him one day what he was looking for in those parts, and Donnán replied: 'I am looking, lord, for a place to stay, where I can serve Christ in pilgrimage'. Ciarán told him to stay there and he would go to some other place, because he knew that this was not to be his place of resurrection. Ciarán then handed over Hareisland with its effects to Donnán, and afterwards came to a place called Ard Manntáin, near the river Shannon. Not wishing to remain in that place, he said: 'I don't wish to stay in a place in which there will be great worldly wealth and merriment. Were I to live here, the souls of my disciples would have difficulty in attaining heaven, for this place belongs to lay people'. Afterwards, Ciarán left that place and came to a place once called [Ard] Tiobrad – now known as Clonmacnoise – and, arriving there, he said: 'Here I shall live, for many souls will go from this place to the kingdom of God, and my resurrection will be here. From then on, Ciarán and his disciples lived there, and he began to build a great monastery, with many coming to him from all over. His parish (*paruchia*) spread out in a great circle, and Ciarán's name was venerated throughout Ireland. A famous and holy monastic town called Clonmacnoise grew in that place in honour of Ciarán; it is located in the western part of the Uí Néill kingdom, on the east bank of the river Shannon, across from the province of Connacht, and both kings and chieftains of the Uí Néill and Connachta are buried there with holy Ciarán. The river Shannon, which is very rich in various kinds of fish, divides the kingdom of Niall, namely Midhe, from the province of Connacht. As Ciarán wished to place with his own hands a corner-post in the first building of the town, a certain druid said to him: 'This is not a good time to begin, for the sign of this hour is contrary to beginnings of buildings'. Ciarán then placed a post in the corner of the building, saying: 'Against your sign, oh druid, I hereby fix this post in the ground, for I care not for the druidic art, and do all my work in the name of my Lord Jesus Christ'. The druid and his followers admiringly praised Ciarán's faith in God.

29 ~ Once, when Ciarán was in Clonmacnoise, some man gave him a fine hooded
       cloak by way of alms, which he then wished to send to the aforesaid holy
       elder Seanán on Scattery Island. However, the way from Ciarán's
       Clonmacnoise in the middle of Ireland to Seanán's Scattery at the mouth of
       the ocean was long, rough and difficult, along the borders of several kingdoms,
       so he could not straightway find someone to take the garment. On Ciarán's
       instructions, the hooded cloak was then placed in the water of the river
       Shannon, and sent off alone until it arrived, still dry, in Scattery and no one
       saw it until it got there. The river Shannon flows namely from Clonmacnoise
       to the estuary at Limerick, where Scattery is located. Filled with the spirit of
       prophecy, Seanán said to his brethren to go to the sea-shore where they would
       find seated a 'guest', a gift from a man of God, and bring it to him. The
       brethren went to the shore without asking any questions and found there the
       bone-dry, hooded cloak, untouched by the waters. Receiving it, the holy elder
       Seanán gave thanks to God and the hooded cloak was with him in revered
       safekeeping, as if a holy diadem.

30 ~ A certain youth of Ciarán's community, called Crithir of Clonmacnoise
       because of his ingenuity, but who was also harmful and impudent, fled from
       Ciarán to the other Ciarán, a most holy aged bishop in the monastic town
       of Seir, which was located in the territory of Éile in the northern part of
       Munster. Staying there with the bishop for some days, he took in his devilish
       way the drink of the brethren and poured it on consecrated fire, thus
       extinguishing it. The elder Ciarán wanted no other fire in his monastery
       except a consecrated one that was never quenched from Easter to Easter.
       When he heard what the young Crithir had done, he was greatly displeased
       and said: 'Let him be put straight by God in this life'. When Crithir heard
       of the holy elder's anger towards him, he left the monastic town of Seir and,
       having gone a short distance away, he was met by wolves and killed, but they
       did not touch his body after his death, as in the case of the prophet who was
       killed by a lion. When the younger Ciarán heard that his boy was with the
       older saint, he set off to visit him and, arriving at Seir on the day of the
       aforesaid events, he was received with due honour. The younger Ciarán then
       said to the older bishop: 'Restore to me alive, holy father, my disciple who
       was killed while here with you'. The older man replied, saying: 'First, your
       feet must be washed, but we have no fire in the monastery with which to heat
       water for you, for, as you know, your disciple quenched the consecrated fire.
       First ask God, therefore, for some consecrated fire'. The younger Ciarán, son

of the carpenter, then extended his arms in prayer to God and, with that, fire came into his lap from heaven, and smoke ascended from the monastery. The older Ciarán then prayed to God on behalf of the youth killed by the wolves and, with that, he arose whole from cruel death, still visibly scarred from the bites of the animals. Blessing all, he took food and drink with the holy men and lived many a day afterwards. The two Ciaráns then established friendship and fraternity in heaven and earth between those who followed after them, and they declared that if someone were to call upon or ask a request of one of them, he should do so of both, and they would hear it. After this, the younger Ciarán, the abbot, said to the older Ciarán, the bishop: 'In your place, father, there will always remain honour and an abundance of riches', to which the older man replied: 'In your place also, dearest son, the vigour of religion and learning will be present until the end of time'. Having said these things and, having received a kiss of peace and a blessing from the older man, the younger Ciarán returned with his followers and the afore-mentioned youth Crithir to his monastic town at Clonmacnoise.

31 ~ One day, when Ciarán's brethren were working at the harvest, they became thirsty through the heat of the sun and sent for cold water to be brought to them. Holy Ciarán replied by a messenger: 'Select, brethren of mine, whether you drink and sate your thirst because of need, or bear with the thirst until evening, so that through your work today in thirst and sweat, future brethren in this place will enjoy abundance and you yourselves will not be without the mercy of God in heaven'. The brethren responded: 'We choose to have sufficiency for those who will follow us, so that we ourselves have the reward in heaven for our patience and thirst'. In this way, the brethren laboured happily that day in thirst, under the boiling sun. When evening came and the brethren returned home, Ciarán wished to please and lovingly refresh them. Trusting in the Lord, he blessed a large vessel full of water, and there, under his hands, a most excellent wine appeared in the vessel. Bringing drinking cups, he instructed the brethren to refresh their bodies soberly while giving thanks to God for his gifts. This was Ciarán's last supper serving his brethren in this life because he lived afterwards for a few days only, and this most abundant supper excelled all other suppers held in the monastery of holy Ciarán, as is shown by this circumstance. After a long time, when Colum Cille and his community had come to Ireland on a visit from the island of Iona, a great supper was prepared for them in Ciarán's monastery at Clonmacnoise. When they came to the monastery, they were received with

great joy and care, and fed most amply at supper, and the fame of that meal was spread widely about the monastery and its surrounds. Some who had separate cells in Ciarán's house were saying, through ignorance, that a supper like this had never been prepared in that place before or after. However, a man who had been there with Ciarán as a youth replied: 'You do not know what you are marvelling at; the supper which our patron Ciarán prepared with water that had been turned into wine for his brethren, thirsty after coming from the harvest, was better by far than this supper. That you may know and believe this, because it is true, come and consider the smell of the thumb with which I drew the wine for the brethren. My thumb touched the liquor over the rim of the vessel in which the wine was drawn, and behold how the odour remains on it'. With all then approaching him, they were satisfied by the pleasant and sweet smell of the holy old man, and they cried out: 'Better by far was that supper whose sweetest odour still remains in the thumb for so long'. Giving thanks to God, they blessed holy Ciarán. In those days, during which Ciarán's brethren were sowing their corn-fields, merchants came to him with wine from Gaul and filled an enormously big vessel with the wine, which the holy man gave to his brethren together with a blessing.

32 ~ Most holy Ciarán, our patron, lived for one year only in his monastic town of Clonmacnoise and, as he knew the day of his death to be approaching, he deplored the evils that would happen in his church in future, but he said that their life would be short. The brethren then said to him: 'What shall we then do, father, in the time of those evils: stay here near your remains or go to other churches'? Ciarán said that they should make haste to other peaceful places and leave behind his remains, like dry bones of a deer on a hill, for it were better for them to be with his spirit in heaven than with his bones on earth in the company of scandal. Holy Ciarán crucified his body greatly, as we shall describe by way of example. He always had under his head a stone pillow which is still today in his monastery, where it is venerated by all. Not wishing to have the stone moved away from him, when he fell ill he commanded that it be placed under his shoulders, so that he might have hardship until death, in anticipation of a perpetual reward in heaven. When the hour of death was already approaching, he commanded that he be brought outside the house and, looking up to heaven, he said: 'This way is arduous, but necessarily so'. At this, his brethren said: 'We know that nothing is difficult for you but at this hour we miserable ones should fear greatly'. Brought back into the house, he raised his hand and blessed his people and clergy and, having received the

Lord's sacrifice, he gave up his spirit on the ninth of September in the thirty-third year of his life. And behold, angels filled the way between heaven and earth, rejoicing in the approach of holy Ciarán. On the third night after Ciarán's death, the most holy abbot Caoimhghin of the province of Leinster came to the funeral. Ciarán spoke to him, and they exchanged garments and established perpetual fraternity between them and theirs. This is faithfully recounted at length in Caoimhghin's Life.

33 ~ When he heard of Ciarán's death, holy Colum said: 'Blessed be God who called most holy Ciarán to him in his youth from out of this life. If he were alive until old age, many would be jealous of him, so great a parish did he acquire in Ireland'. Colum made a hymn for Ciarán and, on showing it himself in Clonmacnoise, Ciarán's successor said: 'This hymn is clear and praiseworthy; what reward may be given to you for it'? Colum replied: 'Give me two handfuls of earth from Ciarán's grave. I desire that, and I shall cherish it more than pure gold and precious gems'. Taking earth then from Ciarán's grave, Colum set off for his island of Iona and, as he was sailing on the sea, a storm arose and the boat was thrust into a whirlpool called in Irish Coire Breacáin. In this, there is a most dangerous marine chasm into which, if boats enter, they do not come out. As the chasm began to draw the boat towards it, Colum threw some of Ciarán's earth into the sea and, very marvellous to relate, at that the storm of the air and motion of the waves ceased to circle around the chasm, which allowed the boat to go a long distance away. Thanking God, Colum then said to his disciples: 'Look, brethren, at how much grace Ciarán's earth brought to us'.

34 ~ While living among men, Ciarán led an angelical life, and the grace of the Holy Spirit shone in his countenance before the eyes of men. Who could tell of his dealings with men in this world? Young though he was in age and body, he was old and most holy in mind and manners, in his humility, mildness, charity, daily actions, nightly vigils, and other divine works. Now, however, he lives in repose without labour; in maturity without old age; in health without pain; in happiness without grief; in peace without an enemy; in abundance without sickness; in everlasting day without night; in a kingdom without end; in front of the judgement seat of Christ, who lives and reigns with the Father and Holy Spirit in the world without end. Amen.

The Life of holy Ciarán, abbot of Clonmacnoise, ends.

The Life of Ciarán of Seirkieran

THE SAINT

THE GENEALOGISTS ATTACHED Ciarán to the Osraighe, the people of Ossory, through his father Luaighne (also written Laighne), reputedly the son of Rumhann Duach of this people's main line of descent.[1] His mother, Liadhain daughter of Maine Cearr, patron of Killyon (Ceall Liadhain) in the parish of Drumcullen, near Seirkieran, and perhaps also of Killeane in the west Cork parish of Kilmoe, was attached to the Corca Laoighdhe, a people of the area now covered by the diocese of Ross in south-west Cork.[2] Her father, Maine, was the eponymous ancestor of a Corca Laoighdhe family named Uí Mhaine.[3] In his person, therefore, Ciarán exemplified the close relationship thought to have existed between the Corca Laoighdhe of south-west Cork and the Osraighe of Ossory, of whom he was the earliest chief patron.[4] This also explains the presence of some of his churches within the diocese of Ross, at Kilkerran and on Clear-island, where, according to the opening chapter of his Life, he was born.

Traditionally regarded not only as Ossory's 'first saint', but also as the first ordained bishop within Ireland as a whole, on the basis that he is said to have been consecrated by the Pope before Patrick ever reached Rome, Ciarán's supposed pre-Patrician status has been shown to belong in the realm of propaganda.[5] Much less prominent among Irish saints than his Clonmacnoise namesake, the annals scarcely notice Ciarán, other than in two eleventh-century references to his successors.[6] He also exercised little influence in Scotland, where dedications to the saint so named refer as a rule to Ciarán of Clonmacnoise.[7] In Cornwall, however, his Life was adapted to serve Piran of

1 *CGSH* §288; Walsh, *Genealogiae*, 93; O'Brien, *Corpus*, 117f3. For the most recent discussion of the pedigree, see Connon, *Territoriality and the cult of Saint Ciarán*, 111–13.   2 O'Donovan, *Miscellany of the Celtic Society,* 21–2; Pender, 'O Clery Book of Genealogies', §2079; *HDGP* vi, 68.   3 Pender, 'O Clery Book of Genealogies', §2079; O'Donovan, *Miscellany*, 19–22; *DIS* 222. Also among Maine's descendants was a saint named Conall who was remembered locally at Tullagh on Sherkin Island.   4 Ibid.; Byrne, *Irish kings and high-kings*, 180; Ó Riain, *Making of a saint*, 84–7.   5 Sharpe, 'Quattuor sanctissimi sancti'. 6 *AFM s.a.* 1048, 1079.   7 Forbes, *Kalendars*, 436; Watson, *The history of the Celtic placenames*, 278.

Life of S. Kieran of Saighir.

Beatissimus episcopus Ciaranus sanctorum Hiberniæ primogenitus i.e. bishop Kieran of *Saighir* was the first saint born in Ireland ; and was of Leinster's eastern portion, which is called Ossory. In that time the Irish all were non-christians and gentiles. *Laighne* was his father's name and he was of the nobles of Ossory ; his mother's name was *Liadain*, and she was of the southern part of Munster, being indeed [to be more precise] of the *Corca-laighde* by race.

---

5. Opening passage of translation of the Life of Ciarán of Seir in S.H. O'Grady, *Silva Gadelica* (London, 1892), ii, 1.

Perranzabuloe and his feast became attached to the like-named Caron of Tregaron in Cardiganshire in Wales.[8]

At home, as can be seen from his Life (§§14, 16), the saint came to be regarded as a prophet, with a prophecy concerning the arrival of the Vikings in Ireland also placed in his mouth.[9] Elsewhere a poem attributed to him extols the virtues of his church at Seirkieran, and an early litany speaks of what may have been a voyage undertaken by him, accompanied by fifteen men.[10] There is no trace of this voyage in his Life.

Ciarán's feast of 5 March, kept locally until modern times at Seirkieran, was observed in many other churches throughout Ossory, including Kilkieran, Rathkieran, Clashacrow, Fertagh, Errill, Knockseera, Tullaherin and Stonecarthy.[11] He shares the feast with his pupil Carthach, patron of the Donegal parish of Kilcar (Ceall Charthaigh), where a well dedicated to Ciarán used to be the scene of an annual pattern.[12] The saint was also patron of Clonsast in the Kildare parish of Kilcock, where he was remembered on 30 April. The parochial church of Kilcock takes its name from Coga, a hypocoristic form of Cóch, the name of Ciarán's foster-mother.[13] According to John O'Donovan, the saint was still venerated in his time throughout the diocese of Ossory, where people swore 'by his hand, *dar láimh Chiaráin*, and by his name, sometimes corrupted to *Parán*'.[14]

The saint's protection continued to be invoked long after his death. At the battle of Dún Bolg in 870, the Osraighe reputedly called upon Ciarán in the

---

8 Orme, *The saints of Cornwall*, 220–1; Ó Riain, 'The saints of Cardiganshire', 388.   9 Knott, 'A poem of prophecies', 60 §9.   10 Meyer, 'Mitteilungen', 13; Plummer, *Irish litanies*, 66.   11 O'Hanlon, *Lives of the Irish saints*, iii, 144. Carrigan, *History and antiquities*, i, 5–16. For a detailed list, see now Connon, *Territoriality and the cult of Saint Ciarán*, 115–20, 150–7.   12 Ó Muirgheasa, 'The Holy wells of Donegal', 147. Carthach is among those who figure prominently in the Life written for Ciarán (§§13, 15, 24, 29).   13 Below §§21, 23.   14 University Library Cambridge, MS Add 622 (1,2) 25.

hope of gaining victory over the Leinstermen, who placed their trust in
Brighid.[15]

Seirkieran can boast of a relatively full record of its abbots from the beginning of
the eighth century through to the late eleventh century.[16] From the late ninth
century onwards, various abbots belonging to an ecclesiastical family known as
Uí Raithnéin – whose pedigrees survive among the genealogies of the Osraighe
– are attested.[17] An earlier abbot, Laidhghnéan mac Doineannaigh, who suffered
a violent death in 744, may have belonged to an Ossory people called Uí Dhuach,
who are treated with respect by Ciarán's biographer.[18]

Among the indications of Seirkieran's continuing importance within Ossory
are the presence there of a round tower – one of two only in Co. Offaly – and
the stump of what appears to have been a large high cross.[19] A late tradition
also indicates that Seirkieran may have been used as a burial place of the kings
of Ossory, at least up to the end of the tenth century, when Donnchadh son
of Ceallach (†975), father of Giolla Pádraig of the main line of Ossory kings,
was buried there.[20] A further measure of Seirkieran's later importance is the
arrival there of the canons regular of St Augustine, most likely during the first
half of the twelfth century.[21] The canons made a point of establishing their
priories near diocesan sees or at places of pilgrimage. Given Ciarán's status as
patron of the diocese of Ossory, Seirkieran may have retained a role in diocesan
affairs for some time after Kilkenny – literally the church of Cainneach (Canice)
– had been chosen as diocesan see.[22] Cainneach, whose Life ignores Ciarán,
is likewise nowhere mentioned in Ciarán's Life.

Ciarán's biographers provided him with no fewer than seven versions of his
Life, first in Latin, then in Irish; the latest of these, a vernacular version compiled

15 Radner, *Fragmentary annals*, §387.   16 Carrigan, *History and antiquities*, ii, 2–3. See also the index to
AFM.   17 O'Brien, *Corpus*, 129b10.   18 *AU, ATig. s.a.*; Sperber, 'The Life of St Ciarán', 134–5; Connon,
Territoriality and the cult of Saint Ciarán, 145–50.   19 Fitzpatrick & O'Brien, *Medieval churches*, 22–3;
AICO §636.   20 Meyer, 'Mitteilungen', 290–1; Carrigan, *History and antiquities*, ii, 7–9. Donnchadh's
grandfather Cearbhall is possibly remembered in a fragmentary inscription on a graveslab at Seirkieran, which
reads: OR DO CHE (*AICO* §636).   21 Gwynn & Hadcock (*Medieval religious houses*, 155, 194–5) place
the foundation before 1170.   22 Ibid., 84–5. See now, Bradley, 'Pulp facts and core fictions'.

probably in the seventeenth century, survives in numerous modern manuscripts.[23] Various dates have been proposed for the original Life of the saint, which is thought by some to have been 'of considerable antiquity'.[24] Two recent detailed studies of the Life have yielded contrasting results. Ingrid Sperber has brought forward arguments in favour of an early date of about the middle of the eighth century, while the present writer has argued in favour of a date in the thirteenth century, when the affiliation of the church to the diocese of Ossory had become a subject of contention.[25]

Once Seirkieran became the location of a priory of regular canons of St Augustine in the twelfth century, the conditions were ripe for the production of a Life of the saint. Thus, when the saint's biographer states in §31 that Ciarán and his namesake at Clonmacnoise joined Bréanainn of Clonfert and his namesake at Birr in establishing 'an eternal community and brotherhood between themselves and between the inhabitants of their monasteries', we need to ask whether these four saints had any association in common at the time of writing.[26] Significantly, of the four churches involved, three, Seirkieran, Clonmacnoise and Clonfert, had become seats of Augustinian houses, probably by the middle of the twelfth century.[27] This also applied to Lorrha, whose patron, Ruadhán, is brought to visit Ciarán, and to Clonard, to whose patron, Finnian, Ciarán is said to have gone to school, although already an old man (§36).[28] It also bears noting that the version of Ciarán's Life recorded by William Carrigan, as 'the living and widespread tradition of Upper Ossory', gave Fertagh, which, like Seirkieran, was the seat of a house of canons, the honour of being the site first occupied by Ciarán.[29] Finally, belonging in the period that followed the arrival of the canons in Seirkieran are historically attested circumstances that could very easily have provided the motivation for the composition of Ciarán's Life.

Since Seirkieran lay in the territory of Éile, well outside the political limits of Ossory, its affiliation to the diocese of Ossory was open to questioning. As

23 See Plummer, *Miscellanea*, 184–5 §20.   **24** Kenney (*Sources*, 316–17), Grosjean ('Vita Sancti Ciarani', 221) and Sperber ('The Life of St Ciarán'), to mention the more important, have all been concerned with the putative, now lost, 'original' text. Kenney described this as a work 'of considerable antiquity', which implies a date well before the twelfth century, and his view was echoed by Grosjean, who used the words 'valde antiqua'. Grosjean, 'Vita Sancti Ciarani', 221.   **25** Sperber, 'The Life of St Ciarán'; Ó Riain, 'The Lives of Saint Ciarán'. Cf. Connon, 'Territoriality and the cult of Saint Ciarán', 149.   **26** Sperber, 'The Life of St Ciarán', 146 § 31a.   **27** Gwynn & Hadcock, *Medieval religious houses*, 164–5, 194–5.   **28** The act of visiting or coming into a person's house was regarded as an act of homage (Murray, 'The dating of Branwen'). Ciarán's visit to Clonard may well imply for the latter church a higher status in the hierarchy of Augustinian houses. This kind of deference is also discernible in the Life of Ruadhán who, while still a boy, is brought to be educated to Finnian of Clonard (Plummer, *Vitae*, ii, 240 §1).   **29** Carrigan, *History*

William Carrigan pointed out, the specification of Slieve Bloom as the western limit of the diocese at the synod of Rathbrassil in 1111 excluded Seirkieran, which lies further west.[30] Not surprisingly, therefore, the church's position within the diocese was eventually contested and, according to an entry in John Clyn's Annals for 1284, the then bishop of Ossory, Geoffrey St Leger (†1286), was forced 'to acquire by combat the manor of Seirkieran'.[31] We may infer from this that the parish of Seirkieran had become a bone of contention at some stage previous to 1284, thus providing the necessary incentive for the composition of Ciarán's Life, arguably in two 'rival' versions.

The Marsh's Library *vita*, the main representative of one group of the saint's Lives, repeatedly emphasizes Ciarán's allegiance to Ossory. It maintains that the saint's origins lay in Ossory, that his father was one of the noblemen of the Osraighe, and that he converted many of his own people of Ossory 'from the error of paganism to the Christian faith' (§§1, 37). This is not the case in the so-called Gotha version of the Life, which became attached to a Cornish saint named Perran.[32] This version establishes a close association between Ciarán and the church of Kildare by the simple expedient of genealogical manipulation. Against the Marsh's Library Life, which assigns Ciarán to the Osraighe, the Gotha Life provides him with a father named 'Domuel/Domnel' (more correctly Domhnall), whose descent corresponds closely to that of a family called the Clann Cholgan.[33] The lands of this family were co-extensive with the barony of Lower Philipstown in east County Offaly, adjoining the present county of Kildare and now forming the northern section of the most western part of the diocese of Kildare.[34] This was Brigidine country; within it, for example, lay Brí Éle, now Croghan Hill, where, according to one tradition, Brighid took the veil.[35]

Saints' biographers usually repeated their arguments under different guises and the author of the Gotha text was no exception. Once more against the evidence of the other Latin Life, he provided Ciarán with a mother named 'Wingela'.[36] Paul Grosjean suggested that the 'impudent hagiographer' (*improbus hagiographus*) had simply invented the name (*ex proprio penu*).[37] However,

and antiquities, i, 8–9. Among other sites allegedly occupied by him on his way to Seir were Errill in the Laois parish of Rathdowney (still part of the diocese of Ossory) and Cooleeshill in the Offaly parish of Corbally. At both places there are wells dedicated to the saint. Cf. Gwynn & Hadcock, *Medieval religious houses*, 176.   30 Carrigan, *History and antiquities*, i, 2.   31 Williams, *The Annals of Ireland*, 152. 32 Orme, *The saints of cornwall*, 220–1; Grosjean, 'Vita S. Ciarani'. Doble, 'The history of the relics'. 33 Grosjean, 'Vita S. Ciarani', 225 § 2, 262 § 42; O'Brien, *Corpus*, 123d35.   34 *HDGP* v, 16.   35 See Ó hAodha, *Bethu Brigte*, xiii.   36 Grosjean, 'Vita S. Ciarani', 225 § 2, 263 § 43.   37 Ibid., 'Vita S. Ciarani', 263n.

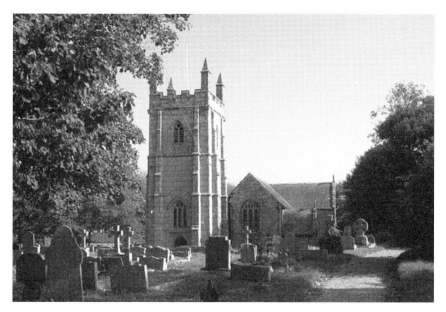

6. Perranzabuloe Church, Cornwall, named from St Piran who was mistakenly taken to be identical with Ciarán of Seir. Photo by Tony Atkin (CC BY-SA 2.0).

the hagiographer is likely to have had an ulterior motive, because he describes Wingela as a daughter of 'Ubdach' (recte *Dubhthach*), thus allowing her to become, as Grosjean also assumes, a sister of Brighid of Kildare.[38]

According to the guidelines laid down at the synod of Rathbrassil, Sliabh Bladhma (Slieve Bloom) served as a northwestern boundary of two dioceses, Ossory and Leighlin.[39] Were similar guidelines to be laid down today, the same mountain range might be cited as a southwestern limit of the diocese of Kildare. Certainly, the western limit assigned to this diocese at Rathbrassil, Rosenallis in the barony of Tinnahinch, Co. Laois, is now well to the east of the actual boundary, which extends far into Co. Offaly, probably as a result of subsequent expansion on the part of the diocese of Kildare.[40] In that case, Ciarán's Lives may have served as documents designed to promote two rival claims to jurisdiction over Seirkieran, one in the interest of the diocese of Ossory, the other favourable to the interest of the diocese of Kildare. Accordingly, the 'original' Life of Ciarán is likely to have been compiled between about 1200 and 1250.

38 Ibid., 263 § 43.   39 MacErlean, 'Synod of Ráith Breasail', 10–11.   40 Ibid., 11.

MANUSCRIPTS AND PREVIOUS EDITIONS

In the ten years or so before William Carrigan published his history of the diocese of Ossory, Ciarán's vernacular Life had already been twice edited, in 1892 by Standish Hayes O'Grady, and in 1895 by D.B. Mulcahy.[41] John Colgan published the *editio princeps* of the Latin version in 1645 in his monumental *Acta sanctorum Hiberniae*.[42] No study has yet been made of the transmission of the late vernacular version, which is preserved in at least ten manuscripts, all dating from later than 1645, but it does not appear to be based on Colgan's edition.[43] Modern scholarly interest in Ciarán's Lives began in 1910 with the critical edition by Charles Plummer of the Marsh's Library text.[44] Plummer was also the first to discuss the interrelationships of the various Lives, Latin and Irish, arranging them in an order which, broadly speaking, still stands.[45] Paul Grosjean published the Gotha version of the Life, of Cornish origin, in 1941, with full commentary, and W.W. Heist provided an edition of the *Salmanticensis* version in 1965.[46] Gilbert H. Doble, who had previously published a summary of the Life in 1931, comparing it with the Cornish version, returned to it in 1942, following Grosjean's edition.[47] Since then, Ingrid Sperber published a translation of the Marsh's Library text in 1998, and the present writer discussed the various Lives of the saint in 2008.[48] Sperber also proposed a division of the extant Lives into two groups, A and B, with the Marsh's Library manuscript at the head of group A and the Gotha Life at the head of Group B.[49] The latter text is closely related to the Irish text edited by Plummer, who designated it the second vernacular Life of Ciarán.[50] The present translation is of the Marsh's Library version of Ciarán's Life, previously translated by Ingrid Sperber.[51]

41 O'Grady, 'Betha Chiaráin tSaighre'; Mulcahy, *Beatha Naoimh Chiaráin Saighre*. Both editions were based on the semi-literal Irish translation of the saint's Latin Life in MT.   **42** Colgan, *Acta sanctorum*, 458–67.   **43** For the manuscripts, see Plummer, *Miscellanea*, 184–5; Grosjean, 'Vita Sancti Ciarani', 218.   **44** Plummer, *Vitae*, i, 217–33.   **45** Plummer, *Vitae*, I, li–liv. Cf. Kenney, *Sources*, 316–17; Grosjean, 'Vita Sancti Ciarani', 217–24; Sharpe, *Medieval Irish saints' Lives*, 391–2; Sperber, 'The Life of St Ciarán', 131–3.   **46** Grosjean, 'Vita Sancti Ciarani'; Heist, *Vitae*, 346–53.   **47** Doble, 'Saint Perran'; idem, 'The history'.   **48** Sperber, 'The Life of St Ciarán'; Ó Riain, 'The Lives of Saint Ciarán'.   **49** Sperber, 'The Life of St Ciarán', 131–3.   **50** Grosjean, 'Vita Sancti Ciarani'; Plummer, *Bethada*, i, 113–24. This version of the Live neglects to mention Ciarán's parents. A full list of manuscripts, editions and translations of the Lives of St Ciarán is in Ó Riain, 'The Lives of Saint Ciarán'.   **51** Sperber, 'The Life of St Ciarán'.

The Life of Ciarán of Seirkieran

THE LIFE OF CIARÁN, BISHOP OF SEIRKIERAN

The Life of holy Ciarán, bishop and confessor, begins

1 ~ Most blessed bishop Ciarán, the first-born of the saints of Ireland, had his origins in the western part of Leinster, the place called Ossory. At the time that he was born all the Irish were pagans. His father Luighne belonged to one of the more noble families of Ossory, whereas his mother Liadhain had her origins in the southern part of Munster, among the family of the Corkalee (*Corca Laoighdhe*). Before she conceived, his mother saw a star fall into her mouth in a dream and, when she told this to wise men, they said: 'You will give birth to a son, a venerable man whose fame and virtue will be known all over Ireland until the end of the world'. Thereafter, Ciarán, the chosen one of God, was conceived, and was born and brought up among the Corkalee, on Clear Island. Truly, then, from his mother's womb, God chose him because, when the name of Christ was still unheard in Ireland, the rigour of the Christian religion began to show itself in him. His parents, and all who saw him, marvelled at his sobriety of mind, natural piety, sweetness of speech, timely fasts, perfect counsels, and all other traits that holy men exhibit.

2 ~ On a certain day, the first of Ciarán's miracles was performed on the aforesaid Clear Island in this way, through divine intervention. While he was still a boy, a kite descended from the sky on a little bird resting on its nest in the presence of Ciarán and snatched it up into the air in its claws. Seeing this misery, the blessed boy was greatly saddened and prayed for the seized bird, upon which its captor returned with the prey and placed it, half-alive and wounded, in front of the boy. Through the grace of God, the miserable little one was straightaway healed under the eyes of this most pious boy whose heart wished it so, and it again rested unharmed on the nest in front of him.

3 ~ Ciarán lived in Ireland in holiness and integrity of body and soul for thirty years, but without baptism, because, as stated already, the Irish were then pagans. Nevertheless, with the Holy Spirit inspiring his servant, Ciarán

behaved both religiously and perfectly and, when he heard of the fame of the Christian religion in the city of Rome, he abandoned Ireland and went there. When he arrived there, he was baptized and instructed in the Catholic faith, and he remained for twenty years, studying the divine scriptures, collecting copies of them, and assiduously learning ecclesiastical rules. When the people of Rome witnessed the wisdom, prudence, religiousness and faith of the man of God, he was ordained a bishop and sent to his homeland of Ireland. On the way in Italy, he met Patrick, archbishop of all Ireland, and, when they saw one another, both rejoiced. At that stage, Patrick was not yet bishop but, afterwards, he was ordained archbishop by Pope Celestine and sent to preach in Ireland. Although there were other holy men there before him, God kept the headship and total archiepiscopacy of Ireland for Patrick, because the kings and chieftains of Ireland did not believe in God through anyone ahead of him. Patrick then said to Ciarán: 'Go to Ireland ahead of me, as far as a well called Fuarán in the centre of the country, on the confines of the northern and southern Irish, and found a monastery there in which there will be reverence and resurrection for you'. When Ciarán replied that he did not know the location of the well, Patrick said: 'Dear brother, you will travel on safely, together with the Lord, and take as a companion on your journey this bell, which will be mute until you arrive at the aforesaid well. When you have arrived there, the bell will find a clear tone and sound sweetly, and I shall come to you there after thirty years'. When the servants of God had kissed and blessed one another, Ciarán went on his way to Ireland while Patrick stayed in Italy. From that day, however, Ciarán's bell remained mute without any sound until he arrived at the well of Fuarán, as Patrick had foretold.

4 ~ When Ciarán arrived in Ireland, God directed him to the well of Fuarán, where the bell of the holy man, called *Bardán Ciaráin*, rang out plainly in a clear sound. The bell is still venerated in Ciarán's monastery and all over his parish. It is carried around the kingdoms for purposes of oath-taking by chieftains, for the defence of poor people, and for the exaction of tribute due to Ciarán's monastery. In truth, the bell was made by bishop Gearmán, Patrick's teacher. As already stated, the well was on the confines of the two parts of Ireland, but south of the line in Munster, in the district called Éile. Blessed pontiff Ciarán began to live there like a hermit, in a wilderness covered by woods. He began to build, first his cell with poor material, then a monastery which grew through the allowance of God and the grace of holy Ciarán, and the whole place was called by the one name of Seir.

5 ~ When holy Ciarán arrived there, he first sat under a certain tree, under the shadow of which was a most ferocious wild boar. When he first saw the man, the terrified boar fled, but God made it tame and it returned as a servant to the man of God, becoming Ciarán's first disciple and, as it were, a monk in that place. This boar, moreover, vigorously cut twigs and hay with its teeth in the presence of the man of God, as material for the construction of the little cell. No one else was with God's holy man up to then, because he had gone off alone from his disciples to the wilds. From there, other animals came to Ciarán from out of their lairs in the wilderness, namely a fox, badger, wolf and hind, and they very tamely remained with him. Like monks, they obeyed the holy man in all, according to his instruction.

6 ~ On another day, the fox, the more cunning and crafty of the animals, stole his abbot's sandals, that is Ciarán's, and, abandoning his vow, took them to his previous lair in the wilderness intending to eat them there. Knowing this, holy father Ciarán sent another monk or disciple, namely the badger, after the fox into the wilderness, in order to lead his brother back to his place. The badger, which was knowledgeable in the woods, went off obediently at the word of its elder and came straight to the cave of its brother fox. Finding the fox about to eat its master's sandals, the badger cut off its two ears and tail, plucked its fur and forced it to come to the monastery and do penance there for the theft. Compelled by necessity, the fox, together with the badger, came at the hour of noon to Ciarán, with his undamaged sandals. The holy man said to the fox: 'Why did you do this evil, brother, which monks ought not to do? Behold our water is sweet and common to all and our food is similarly shared among all. And if you wished by nature to eat flesh, Almighty God would make it from the bark of trees for you on our behalf'. Asking for forgiveness, the fox did penance while fasting, and did not eat again until the holy man ordered it to do so. From then on, it remained with the others as part of the family.

7 ~ After that, his disciples and many others came together in that place from all over, and this led to the beginning of a great monastery. During their lifetime, the afore-mentioned tame animals remained there because it gave the holy elder pleasure to see them. Meanwhile, the Christian faith grew in Ireland because the other three pre-Patrician saints were preaching there, namely Bishop Ailbhe here and there in different places, Bishop Iobhar in the same fashion, and most blessed bishop Déaglán among his own people, the Déise.

Holy Ciarán converted to the faith many from roundabout and many more of his own people of Ossory. Then the glorious archbishop Patrick, who was sent by Pope Celestine, arrived in Ireland and, through the grace of God, converted to Christ kings, chieftains, other rulers and people, so that all Ireland was filled by the faith and baptism of Christ.

8 ~   Ciarán's mother Liadhain, who became a faithful Christian and holy servant of Christ through her son, came to him. He built a cell for his holy mother in a nearby place and brought holy virgins to her there. Among these was a very beautiful girl named Broineach, the daughter of some Munster chieftain, whom the mother of the holy man of God loved dearly, because she was her disciple and upright in manners. When he heard tell of the beauty of the virgin, Díoma, chieftain of the region of Uí Fhiachach, came with his warriors and dragged her away by force from her cell. She was in his fort for many days, sleeping with him as a wife, and he loved her greatly. Ciarán subsequently went off to visit the chieftain Díoma in quest of his disciple, but the man did not wish to release her, by any means or for any reason. He said mockingly to the man of God: 'I shall never release the girl, unless the sound of a stork wakes me from sleep at the break of day tomorrow'. It was then harsh winter and that night a great snow fell but not a snowflake came down in the place where Ciarán and his disciples were. As dawn broke, although contrary to nature, but by the will of God, a stork sounded on the rooftop of each house in the fort. On seeing this, the chieftain Díoma came, prostrated himself in front of holy Ciarán, and released his disciple who was now pregnant. When Ciarán noticed that the female's womb was swelling with child, he blessed it with the sign of the cross, at which her belly decreased in size and the foetus disappeared. The holy man then returned, taking her with him to her church, called in Irish Ceall Liadhain.

9 ~   Afterwards, however, this chieftain Díoma was once more so possessed of love for the young woman Broineach that he came to take her away again. According to the will of all three, however, namely most blessed Ciarán, his holy mother and the young woman Broineach herself, God made it so that the chieftain found her dead, having died there, moreover, as she heard him coming. Seeing her dead, the chieftain was greatly saddened and gloomily said to Ciarán: 'Why did you kill my wife? She was my proper wife, for nobody else but I knew her intimately, and I decreed her to be my spouse forever. For this, you shall not dwell here, Ciarán, because I shall expel you'. The holy man

replied: 'You have no power over me, for God gave you earthly power from above as if it were a shadow, for as long as he might wish, and for this reason I shall be in this place against your will'. When he heard these words, the chieftain angrily and sadly withdrew along the road, while threatening God's servant. God quickly avenged this offence on the chieftain who, on returning to his fort, found it in flames and his beloved son forgotten asleep in his bed. He was only a little boy and, when no one could help him, his nurse said in a loud voice: 'Son, I commend you into the arms of holy Ciarán of Seir'. What a great and marvellous miracle God did there. With the fire put out and the houses consumed by it, that son was found by the men unharmed and unhurt. Seeing this, the chieftain came with bishop Aodh to Ciarán and did penance, promising to carry out anything the holy man would say to him. He offered his two sons to Ciarán, namely Dúnchadh who was saved from the fire and the other one with his seed, to be buried with the saint for all time. Afterwards, the chieftain went back joyously with the man of God's blessing. Sorrowing because his disciple Broineach had departed from this life so quickly, and knowing that the chieftain would not use force on her again, Ciarán went to where her body lay and, praying over her, raised her from the dead. She lived in her professed state for many a day afterwards.

10 ~ One day the prior of Ciarán's monastery came to him to say that they lacked pigs and should purchase some. Ciarán replied that God who gave them other food would also provide pigs. At the saint's word, a very fine sow with twelve piglets, sent by God, was seen on the following day, and from its issue came many herds of pigs.

11 ~ On another day, the prior said to Ciarán that they had no sheep and that they ought to buy some. Ciarán replied that he who gave them pigs would also provide sheep. Going out from the courtyard gate, the prior saw twenty-seven white sheep grazing, likewise sent by God, which similarly grew into flocks.

12 ~ A certain powerful man named Fiontan brought his dead son Laoghaire to Ciarán, to ask that he raise him from the dead in Christ's name. Trusting in Christ, the holy man approached him and, raising him from the dead, gave him back alive to his father. The boy lived for long afterwards, and Ciarán was given a homestead called Ráith Fheara, together with its lands.

13 ~ In the meantime, holy Patrick, who preached to the Irish, came to the kingdom of Munster, where the province's king, Aonghas son of Nad Fraoich in the

royal seat of Cashel, believed and was baptized. A certain man of the Uí Dhuach of Ossory, Mac Eirc by name, killed Patrick's horse without intending to do so. Apprehended by king Aonghas's soldiers, he was put in chains, to be killed but, on being asked by his friends, Ciarán came and gave the king a large amount of gold and silver on his behalf. Now freed, the young man returned to his own kingdom and, once he had gone away, the gold and silver vanished. The furious king summoned Ciarán and asked him why he had given him this apparition in payment for the man. The holy man replied to the king: 'All metals made from nothing will return to nothing'. Angry and threatening, the king was then struck blind by divine punishment and fell to the ground, but Carthach, Ciarán's disciple, who was a nephew of king Aonghas, pleaded greatly with God's holy man on behalf of the king. The man of God said: 'Through his power he sought gold and he will suffer punishment unto death'. The king almost expired but, with the aforesaid Carthach and others pleading for him, Ciarán approached him, caused his sight to return and, as witnessed by some, brought him back to life. Some said, moreover, that the king was dead but, once healed, he gave Ciarán many gifts while thanking God.

14 ~ Aonghas, king of Munster, had excellent harpists who used sweetly sing songs about heroic deeds in his presence, with accompaniment of the harp. Once, as they walked in the district known as Múscraighe Tíre in the kingdom of Munster, they were killed by the king's enemies, and their bodies were hidden in some lake in the wilderness because, during Aonghas's reign, a firm peace was in place over the province. Their harps were then hung from some tree on the edge of the lake. Having no knowledge of what had befallen the harpers, Aonghas was sad but, knowing that Ciarán was full of the spirit of prophecy, he came to him to find out what had happened. Having become a Christian, he did not wish to ask this of druids or soothsayers. Ciarán said to the king: 'Your harpists, lord king, have been secretly killed, their bodies hidden in a lake and their harps hung from a nearby tree'. At the king's request, the holy man Ciarán came with him to the lake and fasted there on that day and, when the fast was over, there was no water visible in the dried-up lake. On seeing the bodies in the depths of the dried lake, Ciarán came to them and, while entreating Father, Son and Holy Ghost as one, he raised them from the dead as if from a deep sleep in the presence of the king and all others. There were seven of them and they had been a whole month dead under the water but, rising up, they took up their harps immediately and sang sweet songs for the

crowds in the presence of king and bishop, and so pleasant was the music that many people fell asleep there, and they gave glory to God with the others. From that day to this, the lake in which they were drowned is dry without water, except that its name is still Loch na gCruitire which, in Latin, is rendered *stagnum cytharedarum* (lake of the harpers). Having received the blessing of king and people, Ciarán then returned to his monastery.

15 ~ One of the stewards of the afore-mentioned king of Munster, who was walking with his companions in the same region of Múscraighe, saw some pigs of a certain man, and ordered his soldiers to kill one. However, when they immediately began to roast the pig in the woods, their enemies fell upon them, and killed that steward with twenty of his men on the bank of the river Brosna. When this was announced to Ciarán, the aforesaid Carthach, the saint's pupil and nephew of Aonghas, persuaded him, with others, to go and bring back the bodies lest wild beasts devour them. When Ciarán noticed that there were too few vehicles to carry the bodies, he announced to the dead men in a loud voice in the presence of all that they, unfortunates ones, should rise up in the name of the Lord Jesus Christ and come with him. At this word, the steward and his twenty men rose up alive and with them the pig they had slain, which then returned to its owner, whose name was Eccanus. All the men thus brought back to life afterwards remained all their lives with Ciarán as religious monks.

16 ~ One day, Ciarán spread a clean cloth over a bush containing many mulberries. Filled with the spirit of prophecy, he foresaw that this would be needed, and he did it so that the berries would be kept mature and sweet for a year, and not harmed by the cold of winter. The berries remained as they were on that day on the bush, or became even better over the year. The following year, Aonghas, king of Cashel, came with his queen to a great feast prepared for him by Conchradh, ruler of Ossory. At the feast the queen fell greatly in love with the aforesaid Conchradh who was very handsome, and commanded him to sleep with her, but on no account did he wish to commit that sin. Knowing this, the queen pretended to be in severe pain, so that she could remain on in the ruler's fort after the king. However, when she was questioned, the queen said that she would be free of the pain if she were now to find mulberries to eat; she thought namely that mulberries could not be found at all at that time. Fearing that she would remain on in his fort after the departure of the king, the chieftain ran off to his holy patron Ciarán, whose parish was

the whole of Ossory, and told him all of this. When he heard this, the bishop sent the chieftain to the bush in the wood, covered by a white cloth and keeping its fruit from autumn until April, and a vessel full of mulberries was brought from there to the queen. When she ate these, she was cured of her pain, namely the love she had for Conchradh because, immediately, she no longer cared for him. The berries were like sweet honey in her mouth and in those of the others eating them. When she saw the miracle wrought on herself, the queen came and, prostrating herself at Ciarán's feet, she confessed her sin to him and sought forgiveness. Sighing, the holy bishop said to her: 'Lady queen, I cannot free you from the death preordained for you, because you, dear daughter, and our lord king will together be killed by your enemies on the same day, but let God show mercy on you'. What the holy priest Ciarán prophesied came to pass. The same king Aonghas was slain on the eighth of October, together with his wife the queen, by the king of north Leinster, Iollann son of Dúnlaing, in a battle on Magh Fé in the province of the Leinstermen, near the great monastic town of Kellistown. This slaughter was a great waste. The queen, Eithne Uathach by name, was a daughter of Criomhthann son of Éanna Ceinsealach, who subjugated the northern part of Leinster, and attained the high kingship of Ireland after he had slain Oilioll Molt, king of Ireland, in the cruel battle of Oiche in the kingdom of Midhe.

17 ~ Once, the holy archbishop Patrick came to Ciarán, together with the king of Munster and nine chieftains, for whom the saint ordered that eight cows and other food be prepared. When he was told that this would not be enough for so many people, he replied: 'Through the grace of God, who satisfied many thousands with a few loaves and fishes, these will also have enough from this moderate amount'. He then blessed the well and excellent wine appeared in it, so that, through the grace of God, there was enough for the archbishop and king with their followers for as long as they were there.

18 ~ On another occasion the king of Tara came with a large host to subjugate the Munstermen, but Oilioll, king of Cashel, was unwilling to assent to this, and went out to give battle to him. When the hosts came together near Ciarán's church, the man of God wished to make peace between them but, being unable to do so, he requested of God what he had failed to get from those proud ones. When they then proceeded from their camps to do battle, the wood between them was torn up from its roots against the Munstermen, according to divine will, and the bed of the river Brosna was raised up as far

as its banks against the king of Tara. When both witnessed this, they were terrified; the king of Tara moved back from the river, which his foot-soldiers and horsemen could previously cross without difficulty, and went off to his own kingdom, while the Munstermen spent the night near Ciarán's monastery. The holy man sent a cooked cow and pig to their king, which was enough for the Munster host, with a residue left behind by them. Through this, Ciarán's fame spread widely.

19 ~ A crowd of thieves once came to the borderlands of Munster from another region to pillage and kill, but a nobleman, Lonán by name, fell on them and they turned back in flight. Despairing of being able to escape, they pleaded with Ciarán to save them and, as Lonán and his followers began to seize them and lay them low, a fiery ball suddenly fell from above, behind their backs but in front of Lonán. Much terrified by this, Lonán and his soldiers, now no longer able to pursue them, retreated, while the others, knowing how the power of God had freed them from great danger by the grace of holy Ciarán, came to the saint and told him what had happened. Having taken counsel, they then became monks of Ciarán and remained under his care, doing good works until they died.

20 ~ Another time, a thief from Leinster by the name of Cairbre took a fine cow by force from Ciarán's monks. When he reached Slieve Bloom, fog and darkness surrounded him and, unable to find the way, he came to a river, fell into it and died. The cow then came back directly to holy Ciarán.

21 ~ The most blessed bishop Ciarán sent oxen without a driver to his foster-mother Cóch (Coinche), and they came by a direct route to the holy woman, who knew that her outstanding pupil Ciarán had sent them to her for ploughing purposes. There was a long way between Ciarán's monastery at Seir and that of Cóch at Rossmanagher, which is located near the western sea of Ireland. The oxen used to plough at Cóch's place each year and, when the ploughing was over, return each year to Ciarán without any human companion.

22 ~ On the night of the Lord's birth, when his followers had received communion from his hand in Seir, Ciarán was accustomed to travel a great distance to the afore-mentioned Cóch's church at Rossmanagher in order to offer up the body of Christ in Cóch's presence on that most holy night. When God's holy

woman had received with others the Lord's communion from his hand, he headed back before dawn to his own monastery of Seir in the middle of Ireland. It is hidden from us, moreover, how he came and went, because he told none of us. We know it, however, because God, who allowed Habakuk to go from Judea to Caldea and return in the short space of a day, carried out for his servant whatever Ciarán wanted.

23 ~ A certain large stone, now called Cóch's stone, on the seashore not far from her church, on which the saint often prayed to the Lord, stood between the waves. Once Ciarán entered the water on that stone and joyously returned to his own church on it. For it is written: 'God is wonderful in his saints'.

24 ~ Ciarán's pupil Carthach, of whom we spoke above, and a certain virgin from the church of Liadhain, Ciarán's mother, had a carnal passion for one another and, driven on by carnal flame, they fell greatly in love with one another. After a while, on a certain day, they arranged a tryst to meet and fulfil their desire for one another. Arriving at the appointed place, and wishing to have intercourse, a ball of fire suddenly came down between them, and almost consumed them, so that, speechless and terrified, they both fled back. That same day the virgin was struck by lifelong blindness, as was proper, for she had blinded her mind through that illicit act, and now did penance through her bodily sightlessness, whereas Carthach became a penitent pilgrim. This befell them through the sanctity of the good shepherd Ciarán who was at all times vigilant in the care of his flock.

25 ~ Two blood brothers named Odhrán and Meadhrán from the territory of Múscraighe Tíre wanted to be pilgrims in another province, namely near Assaroe in the kingdom of Connacht. Their place was called Latteragh and, when they came to Ciarán at Seir, Meadhrán wished to stay there, only to have his brother say that this was not what he had promised, and he asked Ciarán not to retain him. Ciarán replied: 'Almighty God will adjudge as to whether he ought to stay here or go with you. While being judged, therefore, let him hold a lamp in his hand and, if this is lit by blowing from his mouth, he ought to stay; if not, let him go with you'. Meadhrán immediately lit the lamp by blowing on it, and remained on with Ciarán in great holiness until his death. Ciarán then said to blessed Odhrán: 'Listen to me, brother, for I say to you that even if you were to visit the four parts of the world, you would still die in your place at Latteragh. Return now, therefore, and stay there, for

that place will be known by your name for ages'. Thus it was done in accordance with Ciarán's word; Odhrán, who became a man of great virtue and holiness, returned to the aforesaid place and constructed a famous monastery there. Then, after performing many miracles, which are to be read in his Life, he moved happily as abbot of that place to the kingdom of heaven and, as was foretold, the place is known by his name as Latteragh of Odhrán.

26 ~ Having carelessly fallen to the ground and fractured her body greatly, a certain lady by the name of Eachall died. Ciarán resuscitated her after three days and the lady bestowed on him a district called Léim Eachaille after her. She and her family gave thanks to God.

27 ~ A steward of the king of Munster by the name of Ceann Faoladh killed Crónán, a friend of Ciarán, whom the aged saint resuscitated in the name of the Lord after seven days. When he had raised him from the dead, the holy elder said in front of all: 'Ceann Faoladh, who unjustly killed this man, will soon be himself slain, and his body burnt by the people of Éile in the fort called Ráith Mhaighe'. Everything turned out in this way.

28 ~ At another time, Oilioll, king of Munster, angrily spoke harsh words against Ciarán, upon which the king departed from the saint. Thereafter, the king was struck dumb and said nothing for seven days. Afterwards, he returned to the elderly Ciarán, prostrated himself at the feet of the man of God and did his will. When he noticed his remorseful heart, the holy man blessed his tongue and there, with his speech restored, the king spoke clearly in the presence of all. Then, having received the blessing of the most holy bishop, the king, marvelling at the divine miracle, went on his way with his followers.

29 ~ One night, the most holy elderly bishop Ciarán lowered himself into a river of cold water together with a certain religious pilgrim named Gearmán. When they had been in the water for a long time, the cold affected the pilgrim so much that he said to the old man: 'Lord father, I cannot put up with the cold of this water any longer'. The bishop then blessed the water with the sign of the holy cross and it showed itself warm about the pilgrim, like water in a bath. Thereupon, as both were praising the Lord, Ciarán said to Gearmán: 'A most dear guest will come to us tomorrow, namely Carthach, son of the king of Cashel, whom I fostered for God since his youth. I sent him on a pilgrimage because of a sin he wished to commit until God prevented it

through me, lest he waste his vow and work, but now, having earned
forgiveness, he will return. Catch, therefore, the fish that is swimming about
you so that my beloved son can be fed with it'. Gearmán then caught the large
fish, as the elder had said, and Carthach arrived on the following day. The
sin namely for which he was sent on pilgrimage, as is read, was when a column
of fire came down between him and a virgin.

30 ~ On another occasion, holy Ciarán, abbot of Clonmacnoise, was made captive
by a king named Furbhaidhe and placed in chains. The king did this because
[the saint], being full of charity, divided among the poor the royal goods that
were in his care. One day, the king said mockingly to Ciarán: 'If you wish to
escape, give me seven shaved cows, red of body but white of head'. 'For God
all things are possible', said Ciarán, 'release me and I will search for such things
for you, or else I will come back once more for your judgement'. Now released
and guided by God, the abbot Ciarán went to the afore-mentioned elder
bishop Ciarán, and told him of all that had happened to him. The two saints
Bréanainn happened to be with the elder bishop Ciarán and all were joyous
at the arrival of abbot Ciarán. Bishop Ciarán then asked his cellarer what he
had to eat for their holy guests, to which the brother responded that he had
nothing but a piece of bacon, and he did not know if they would eat it. The
holy elder said to him to prepare it quickly for them to eat and, when cooked,
Ciarán came and blessed it, at which point it became in the presence of the
brethren curds and pottage, fish, honey and oil; and wine a-plenty in small
vessels appeared at that meal through the Lord's divine largesse. There was a
certain former layman by the name of Mac Conghail present at that meal
who did not wish to eat with the holy men, saying that he would certainly
not eat food made from bacon. Bishop Ciarán said to him: 'You will eat meat
for sure during Lent and on that day you will be slain by enemies and
decapitated, and the kingdom of heaven will not be yours. Once your habit
is discarded you will live unhappily'. All these things came to pass and the
layman was killed on the lands of the monastic town of Seir.

31 ~ Thereupon, those four saints, the two Ciaráns and two Bréanainns, signed
up to a friendship and fraternity between themselves and between the
occupants of their churches forever. Having received the permission and
blessing of the other holy fathers, abbot Ciarán set off on his way, still not
knowing where to find the cows he ought to deliver to the king. The most
blessed elder priest, bishop Ciarán, set off with the younger Ciarán in order

1 Aerial view of Clonmacnoise, incorporating remains of the medieval monastic site and adjoining Anglo-Norman castle (© Joe O'Sullivan).

2 Beginning of the Life of Ciarán of Clonmacnoise in Dublin, Marsh's Library MS Z.3.1.5, fol. 144, with genealogy of the saint added in the bottom margin; by permission of the Governors and Guardians of Marsh's Library (© Marsh's Library).

3 *(opposite)* Cross of the Scriptures, Clonmacnoise (courtesy of Roger Stalley). The two figures in the lower panel on the east face of the cross have sometimes been taken to represent Ciarán and a king beginning to construct the church (Harbison, *High crosses*, i, 49 E 1; Rekdal, 'Memorials', 116–17, 120–1).

4 Two views of the monastic site at Seirkieran (*top*, by James Fraher for Offaly County Council; *bottom*, by Caimin O'Brien). The upper view includes remains of the Augustinian priory.

5 Beginning of the Life of Ciarán of Seirkieran in Dublin, Marsh's Library MS Z.3.1.5, fol. 106; by permission of the Governors and Guardians of Marsh's Library (© Marsh's Library). Diarmuid Ó Riain (pers. comm.) has identified the hand of the note in the left margin as that of Meredith Hanmer who repeated the wording in English in his *Chronicle of Ireland*, p. 72.

6 Aerial view of the site of Colmán's church at Lynally, photographed by Caimin O'Brien.

7 *(opposite)* High Cross at Castlebernard, near Kinnitty (courtesy of Roger Stalley). The figure holding a crosier in the centre panel has been taken by Margaret Stokes to represent Fíonán (Harbison, *High crosses*, i, 36 S 2).

8 Inisfallen church, Lower Lake, Killarney (courtesy of Roger Stalley). This was the most important of the Kerry churches dedicated to Fíonán, and much of the detail in the saint's Life may have come from its scriptorium.

to lead him along a certain part of the route where, blessing one another, they decreed between them on each side an exchange of blessings. The younger Ciarán said to the older: 'Father, there will always be an abundance of riches in your church'. The older Ciarán responded: 'Son, an abundance of wisdom and religion will always remain in your church'. These prophecies of the holy men have since come to completion. When they had come from there to a place called Áth Salchair, they found seven hairless cows, red-bodied and white-headed. 'Behold', said the older Ciarán, 'how God has given us cows that ought to be given back to the king'. Giving praise to God, the servants of Christ then parted with a blessing and kiss of peace, the older Ciarán returning to Seir, the younger going back to the king to give him the cows. The king and those with him marvelled greatly as to how the holy man could obtain the likes of them, but when Ciarán, now free, retired from the king's presence, those animals were no longer visible. The king then knew that he had acted unfairly.

32 ~ In the monastery of abbot Ciarán at Clonmacnoise, there was a certain boy called Críchidh Cluana, harmful to the good and more so to the wicked. This boy once came to the monastery of Seir, and stayed for some days with the elder bishop Ciarán. The old bishop decided that the consecrated Easter fire of his monastery was not to be extinguished for a year. Prompted by the devil, the boy knowingly extinguished the fire, upon which Ciarán said to the brethren: 'Behold, our consecrated fire has been put out by this accursed boy Críchidh, who is always accustomed to do harm. There will be no fire in this place until next Easter unless it be sent by God. However, Críchidh, who put out the fire, will be killed tomorrow'. The following day he was killed by wolves in the countryside and lay there dead. On hearing about this, the younger Ciarán, to whom the boy belonged, came to the monastery of the elder Ciarán at Seir and was received with honour. There was no fire in the monastery because all fires there used to be lit daily from the consecrated fire, and the saint had undertaken that there would be no fire there unless God sent one, so the guests were cold on that snowy day. On seeing this, the elder Ciarán rose and spread out his arms in prayer to the Lord, and a ball of fire fell from above into his lap, which the holy bishop first carried in his cloak to the guests and, once these had become warm, a supper was brought to the tables. When they sat at table, abbot Ciarán declared in the presence of all that he would not eat until his boy, who had been killed there, came to him alive. The older Ciarán then said: 'We know therefore why you came, and

God will breath life into him on our behalf. Eat then and your boy will hurry here'. The boy then quickly came and ate with the brethren, and all raised a clamour in praise of God and in acclaim of his saints. Afterwards, the younger Ciarán, having received the blessing of the older man, returned with his boy to his community.

33 ~ At another time, one of the brethren, Baoithín by name, carelessly extinguished a fire early on and, sorrowing greatly, sought forgiveness. On that day, holy Ruadhán, abbot of Lorrha, came to visit Ciarán, but there was no fire in the monastery of Seir by which the guests might be warmed and a meal prepared for them. Knowing this, Ciarán blessed a nearby stone, which lit up with fiery flames. Taking the stone in his hands, the man of God then carried it to Ruadhán and his companions who, on seeing this, rejoiced and were strengthened in God.

34 ~ The aforesaid Baoithín again carelessly spilled a vessel full of milk on the ground, but the holy elder Ciarán blessed the vessel with the sign of the cross and, in the presence of all, it became full of excellent, hitherto unknown milk. In awe of their most holy master, the brother who spilled it and the other brethren were confirmed in their love of God.

35 ~ A few days before his death, as the most holy but now weak elder priest Ciarán was praying, an angel of the Lord appeared to him. The saint then asked three requests of God in the angel's presence. With divine permission, the angel promised him these, as follows: hell would not close after the Day of Judgement over those who were buried in the graveyard near his cathedral church; whoever would honour the feastday of his birth would be rich and have future repose, and the people of Ossory, who accept him as patron, should not lay waste any other people by moving out of their own territory into another and calling it to battle. However, if another people were to enter their territory unlawfully, wishing to lay it waste, never should the forces of Ossory be defeated in battle in their own territory. God promised these three petitions to holy Ciarán before he died.

36 ~ This holy man, namely Ciarán, was very humble in every way; he loved greatly to hear and learn divine scripture up until his feeble old age. It is said of him that he with other Irish holy men of that period went in old age to the most holy and wise Finnian, abbot of the monastery of Clonard, and studied divine

scripture in his school. For this reason, Ciarán, like other holy men of Ireland, is said to have been a pupil of Finnian's. Out of humility and love of learning, this wise and blessed elder, as well as bishop, was prepared to learn at another's knee.

37 ~ Unbelievably, from youth onwards until his death, most blessed Ciarán made do without soft clothes, meats, inebriating drinks, sleep, and other delights of the flesh. He also converted his people of Ossory and many others from the error of paganism to the Christian faith. Miraculously, he was also the subject of frequent visits of angels. He ordained an innumerable multitude of bishops, priests and other holders of ecclesiastical positions.

38 ~ In a certain place, our holy patron Ciarán sought a well, which an angel of the Lord marked out for him. Now called Ciarán's well, many sick people are healed through its water and the grace of the man of God.

39 ~ Most holy Ciarán lived for three hundred years in the flesh, in devoted service of God before and after baptism. When he became infirm with old age and suffering, and knowing the day of his death, he called his community to him and, blessing them, recommended to them God's commands. Then, on the fifth of March, having received the holy sacrament, he set free his happy soul in the peace of Christ and among choirs of saints. On the same night by their own will and through God's providence, thirty holy bishops ordained by Ciarán passed over into the kingdom of Christ, where there is honour and glory with God the father and the Holy Ghost in all eternity. Amen.

Thus ends the Life of holy Ciarán bishop and confessor.

The Life of Colmán of Lynally

THE SAINT

THE EARLIEST MENTION OF COLMÁN is in Adhamhnán's late seventh-century Life of Colum Cille, which speaks of his two sea passages between Ireland and Iona. One of these saw him traverse the 'surging tides' of the whirlpool of Breacán, near Rathlin Island, while the other resulted in Colum Cille drawing attention to his own imminent death.[1] Adhamhnán was the first to record Colmán's attachment to the Maca Seille (Sailne), which is also attested in some annal notices of his death.[2] The Dál Seille were a rent-paying people (*aitheachthuath*) of Dál nAraidhe, with lands in Antrim between Dál nAraidhe and Dál mBuain, now corresponding to the district about Connor in south Antrim.[3] They traced their origins variously to Conaing son of Eacha and Feidhlimidh Seille, a brother of Feidhlimidh Buan, ancestor of the Dál mBuain.[4] Later, Colmán is more usually assigned to the descendants of Eacha son of Muiridh of north-east Ulster, through a father named Beoghain.[5] Among other saints belonging to this group was Mac Nise of Connor whose Life foretells the occupancy of Lynally by his relative Colmán. According to the genealogists, Seanán of Laraghbryan and Maol Ruain of Tallaght also belonged to the family.[6] Both Connor and Laraghbryan enjoyed a close association with Lynally through joint abbacies in the period 770–1050.[7]

Saints' pedigrees were often subject to the demands of local or provincial politics, both ecclesiastical and secular. Colmán's descent was later influenced by provincial loyalty, as is clear from the opening sentence of the Latin Life translated below (§1), which claims him for the Uí Néill, the dominant kindred in the Northern Half of Ireland. On the other hand, his Irish vernacular Life (*beatha*), while acknowledging his northern descent, places great emphasis on

---

1 Anderson & Anderson, *Vita Columbae*, 222, 356–8. For a detailed discussion of Colmán's genealogical record, see Charles-Edwards, 'Érlam', 282–4; cf. idem, *Early Christian Ireland*, 61–4. 2 *ATig. s.a.* Cf. *CS*; *AFM*; *MartT* 74. 3 *HDGP* vii, *s.v.* (forthcoming). 4 O'Grady, *Silva Gadelica* i, 234; Ó Muraíle, *Leabhar Mór*, 102.2/102.4. 5 *CGSH* §311, Walsh, *Genealogiae*, 95; cf. Ní Dhonnchadha, 'The beginnings', 560–1. 6 Heist, *Vitae*, 406 §14. 7 See p. 54.

¹DE BAITHENEO ET COLUMBANO FILIO ²BEOGNIª, SANCTIS PRESBYTERIS, EADEM SIBI DIE VENTUM PROSPERUM A DOMINO PER BEATI VIRI ORATIONEM DONARI POSTULANTIBUS, SED DIVERSA NAVIGANTIBUS VIA.

³ALIO quoque in tempore, superius ⁴memoratiᵇ sancti viri ad ⁵Sanctum venientes, ab eo simul unanimes ⁶postulant ut ipse a Domino ⁷postulans ⁷impetraret prosperum crastina die ventum sibi dari diversa emigraturis via. Quibus Sanctus respondens, hoc dedit responsum, ⁸Mane crastina die, ⁹Baitheneus, a portu ¹⁰Iouæ enavigans insulæ, flatum ¹¹habebit secundum usquequo ad portum perveniat Campi ¹²Lungeᶜ. Quod ita, juxta Sancti verbum, Dominus donavit: nam ⁹Baitheneus plenis eadem die velis magnum totumque pelagus usque ad ¹³Ethicam transmeavit terramᵈ. ¹⁴Hora vero ejusdem diei tertia, vir venerandus Columbanum ¹⁵advocat presbyterumᵉ dicens, Nunc Baitheneus

7. Late seventh-century mention of Colmán (*Columbanus filius Beogni*) in W. Reeves, *The Life of St Columba … by Adamnan* (Dublin, 1857), p. 124.

the local families associated with his church, the O'Molloys (Uí Mhaolmhuaidh) lords of Fir Cheall, whose lands included the area about Lynally, and the descendants of Cuinneagán and Duineacha, who were the saint's local devotees.[8]

Regardless of what the genealogists had to say of Colmán's origins, he may ultimately have been identical with his namesake Colum Cille. His mother Mór, for example, is said by Colmán's vernacular biographer to have been Colum Cille's sister.[9] Colmán was also one of three bearers of the name attached to a small triangle of Midland churches, who are said to have acted on behalf of Colum Cille, when the latter went into exile.[10] The two others were the patrons of Lynn, near Mullingar, and Conry in the Westmeath barony of Rathconrath.[11] The feastdays of all three bring them close to Colum Cille. Colmán of Lynn was remembered on 17 June, the octave of the feast of Colum Cille, while the feasts of the saints of Conry and Lynally respectively fell on 25 and 26 September. The former September date coincides with the feast of Finbarr of Cork, while the latter is the vigil of the feast of a bishop Finnéan, both of whom are arguably localizations of Finnian alias Fionnbharr, Colum Cille's teacher.[12]

Colmán's relative importance in the hagiographical record is shown by the notice of his birthday on 3 October – the octave of his main feast – in two early ninth-century martyrologies kept at Tallaght, and in a calendar from the

8 Plummer, *Bethada*, i, 168–9 §§1–8.   9 Ibid., 168 §4; ii, 347 §23.   10 O'Kelleher & Schoepperle, *Betha Colaim Chille*, 212 §219.   11 *DIS* 186–7, 196–7.   12 Ó Riain, *Making of a saint*, 19–23.

same period kept by an Irishman on the Reichenau in Lake Constance.[13] The saint was noted for his learning; an early instructional tract entitled *Aibghitir Chrábhaidh* ('Alphabet of Piety') is attributed to him in several manuscripts, but his authorship is the subject of much debate.[14] A subject of much less debate is the attribution to him of a hymn in praise of Patrick (*Hymnus Patricii*) in a gloss to Tíreachán's seventh-century Life of Patrick, which James Carney took to have more authority than the usual attribution to Secundinus, alias Seachnall.[15] The ninth-century Tripartite Life of Patrick attributes to Colmán the recital of a hymn in praise of the Armagh saint, as does the text of his own Life along much the same lines (§33).[16]

Among other saints' Lives that feature Colmán are those of Finnian of Clonard, Mochuda of Rahan, Mochua of Timahoe, and Ruadhán of Lorrha. In Finnian's Life a section corresponding closely to the account in Colmán's Life (§49) of the sequel to Finnian's death follows the passage which lists the virtues of the Clonard saint.[17] Mochuda was patron of Rahan, which adjoins Lynally, and Colmán plays a critical role in his Life, directing Mochuda to the location of his church and subsequently blessing its cemetery.[18] The church of Killeshin instead of Lynally forms the backdrop to Colmán's mention in the Life of Mochua of Timahoe. Described as a 'noble and wise' man, Colmán allegedly visited Mochua in search of the knowledge he had previously held, which, after he had failed to interpret a verse sung by a heavenly bird, he went on to re-acquire through the expulsion of an 'unclean spirit' dwelling in him.[19] Finally, in Ruadhán's Life, a hind milked at Lorrha is described as then hurrying to Lynally, where it was milked on the following day.[20]

Colmán became patron of several other churches beside Lynally. His ancestral connections with the district about Lough Neagh led to his adoption as patron in three Antrim churches: Ahoghill where, in contrast to his more usual Columban associations, he was thought to have been one of Patrick's priests; Connor, where, according to the Marsh's Library version of his Life, he was 'second patron' after Mac Nise, and Muckamore.[21] Devotion to the saint also extended to churches in Scotland, including two named after him, Colmonell in Ayrshire and Kilcolmonell in Kintyre. The latter place is probably the church in Kintyre granted to him, according to his vernacular Life, by the

---

13 *MartT* 76; *MartO* 214; Schneiders, 'The Irish calendar', 60.   14 Hull, 'Apgitir Chrábaid', 49–50.
15 Carney, *The problem*, 40–6.   16 Mulchrone, *Bethu Phátraic*, ll. 2906–9.   17 Heist, *Vitae*, 106–7 §35.   18 Plummer, *Vitae*, i, 177 §19, 180 §29.   19 Plummer, *Vitae*, ii, 184 §2.   20 Plummer, *Vitae*, ii, 250 §2r; Ó Riain, *Four Tipperary saints*, 83 §24.   21 McKay, *Placenames of Northern Ireland*, iv, 158–61; Plummer, *Vitae*, i, 259 §3; Reeves, *Ecclesiastical antiquities*, 98.

Scottish king for having rid the area of a terrifying monster.[22] Closer to Lynally, he was associated with two Leinster churches: Killeshin in Co. Laois and Tullaghanbrogue in Co. Kilkenny.[23]

According to the annals, Colmán died in 611 at the age of fifty-five.[24] His crozier was apparently still kept as a relic at Lynally in the early seventeenth century, and the saint's cross used to be invoked as a protection against being thrown from a horse.[25]

THE CHURCH

The *Salmanticensis* version of the saint's Latin Life (§14), which is translated below, states that Lynally was founded as the result of an appeal by Colum Cille to Aodh son of Ainmhire (†598) and Aodh Sláine (†604), successive kings of the Uí Néill. Aodh Sláine, we are told, invited the saint to choose a site in a wood named Fiodh Eala in the southern part of his kingdom, where Colmán, accompanied by Colum Cille's steward, Laisréan of Durrow, selected a suitable place. From this account, it would appear that Lynally was considered at the time to be closely affiliated to the Columban church of Durrow, of which Laisréan was patron.[26] The parishes of Lynally and Durrow are now separated by one parish only. Moreover, the church that gave name to the neighbouring parish of Rahan, which adjoins both Lynally and Durrow, is said to have been located at a place where Colum Cille first thought of building his own church.[27] Rahan's patron Mochuda – having been allegedly directed to the place by Colmán Eala – is said to have used three bundles of wattles left behind by Colum Cille with which to build his church.[28]

The vernacular Life of the saint gives the O'Molloys (Uí Mhaolmhuaidh) the honour of assigning Lynally, then the home of a harmful wild animal, to Colmán, before going on to identify a local family named Muintir Chuinneagáin as the saint's hereditary stewards.[29] Present at the founding of the church were also, according to this text, several other saints, all of whom are otherwise omitted from mention in the Life.[30] Despite being one of Ireland's three most famous fairs and a haven of Ireland's chastity, Lynally cannot be said to have attracted a great deal of attention in the Irish annals.[31] The Annals

---

22 Plummer, *Bethada*, i, 175–6 §26.   23 Plummer, *Vitae*, ii, 184 §2; Carrigan, *History and antiquities*, iii, 385.   24 *AU s.a.*; *ATig. s.a.* Cf. *MartT* 74.   25 *MartD* xliv; Meyer, 'Irish quatrains', 455.   26 *DIS* 389. 27 Plummer, *Vitae*, i, 177 §20.   28 *Ibid.*   29 Plummer, *Bethada*, i, 168–9.   30 Ibid., i, 169 §8; ii, 346 §8. 31 Meyer, *Triads*, §§31, 35. Less favourable commentary occurs in Triad §44, which describes the church as one of 'three unlucky places in Ireland'. See also Charles-Edwards, *Early Christian Ireland*, 556–7.

Acta Sancti Colmani Elo.

Incipit vita Colmani Elo.

1. FUIT vir vite venerabilis, nomine Colmanus, filius Beugne, de nepotibus Neill, qui de vocabulo cujusdam silve, que dicitur Alo, augmentum [1] nominis accepit. Hujus Colmani parentes in tempore cujusdam vastationis hostilis cum ceteris civium turbis in fugam versi sunt, et pervenerunt in vallem Hoichle ; et dum ibi essent, impleti[2] sunt dies ut mater illa pareret. Cumque advenisset hora partus illius, [unus][3] de assistentibus apprehendit lignum cujusdam vichiculi quod erat valde aridum, et roboris illiusque ligni fastigium in terram fixit, et e contra radicem sursum erexit, ut sicut feminis mos est, in tempore parturiendi illud lignum in suis manibus mater teneret et sic pariet. Postqua mautem mater genuit sanctum filium, lignum istud aridum,

Kannecho Coimano, ut ab ipso instrueretur in doctrina sacra et moribus sanctis. Huic Coimano [4] quedam sancta femina ministrabat. Que quadam die vaccas mulgens, ira repentina movebatur adversus sanctum puerum Colmanum sibi ministrantem, ita[5] ut de lora[6] qua pedes vaccarum colligantur manu sua sinistra caput pueri percuteret. Cumque ad domum reversi essent, senex Coimanus increpavit illam dicens : *Quare lesisti puerum? Quasi hominem ministrantem tibi vides, et tamen Deum in corde ejus non vides. An nescis quod Dominum in templo sancto suo sedentem offendisti et sanctos angelos ejus?* Illa autem audiens hec verba, lacrimis et fletibus penitentiam egit. Quod cum vidisset senior, ait illi : *Suscepit Deus penitentiam tuam. Dei exspecta judicium. Cras enim vindictam a Deo recipies.* Crastino autem die manus ejus sinistra, qua puerum percussit, nudos angulos continuet

8. Opening passage of the first modern edition of Colmán's Life in C. de Smedt & J. de Backer, *Acta sanctorum Hiberniae ex codice Salmanticensi nunc primum integer edita* (Edinburgh & London, 1887), col. 415.

of the Four Masters, which has the widest coverage of all the annals, records ten abbots over a period of 300 years, beginning with an otherwise unknown St Bran in 735 and ending at 1038 with Cuinnidhéan, a bishop, abbot and teacher.[32] Most noteworthy about the obits of these abbots is the fact that nine of the ten held joint abbacies of Lynally and Connor in the period between 773 and 1038. Indeed one abbot, Tiobraide (†896) by name, is said to have held three headships, of Lynally, Connor and Laraghbryan in Co. Kildare. As already stated, Colmán was allegedly 'second patron' of Connor, and the principal patron, Mac Nise, is among the saints assigned, with Colmán, to the Dál Seille family.[33] Moreover, Ahoghill in Co. Antrim, of which Colmán was patron, adjoins Connor. Cuinnidhéan (†1038), the final 'coarb of Mac Nise and Colmán Eala' noticed in the annals, may have been the progenitor of the

32 *AFM* s.a.   33 Walsh, *Genealogiae*, 96–7. Cf. Charles-Edwards, *Early Christian Ireland*, 61–7.

family known as Muintir Chuinneagáin, which, as already pointed out, later provided *maoir*, 'stewards', of Lynally.[34] The Life states that this family was a branch of the Uí Bhriúin of Connacht.[35]

THE LIFE

Colmán's Latin Life, which, while ignoring other indications of descent, opportunistically assigns the saint to the powerful Uí Néill, forms part of the so-called O'Donohue group in the *Codex Salmanticensis* whose texts have been dated by some scholars to as early as the eighth century.[36] There are many features of these Lives, however, that point to the influence of the canons regular of St Augustine whose first foundation in Ireland dates to the 1130s.[37] In Colmán's case, this is perhaps no more than might be expected of a text relating to a church located within a few miles of Durrow, where an Augustinian priory was founded, possibly already in the 1140s, by Murchadh Ua Maoil Sheachlainn, king of Midhe.[38] By arranging for Laisréan, 'Colum Cille's steward' (§14) and superior of Durrow, to accompany Colmán as he chose the location of his church, the author of the saint's Life all but conceded that Lynally was affiliated to the Columban (later Augustinian) church.[39] A second church of which Colmán was patron, at Muckamore in Antrim, near Lough Neagh, was also to become the site of an Augustinian priory.[40]

The lateness of the Life may also be indicated by the mention in §20 of the 'school of John the Evangelist' in Rome, which can only refer to a school at the *omnium urbis et orbis ecclesiarum mater et caput*, 'the mother and head of all the churches of city [of Rome] and the world', St John Lateran.[41] Primarily dedicated to Christ the Saviour, the basilica was rededicated to John the Baptist in the tenth century, and dedicated once more in the 1140s to John the Evangelist during the papacy of Lucius II (†1145), a canon regular of the church of San Frediano in Lucca.[42] The context relates to news brought from Rome of the death of Pope Gregory, and an awareness of the rededication of

---

34 Plummer, *Bethada*, i, 169 §10.   35 Ibid. 168 §1.   36 Sharpe, *Medieval Irish saints' Lives*, 329, 384; Herbert, 'Literary sea-voyages', 182–9.   37 Ó Riain, 'The O'Donohue Lives'.   38 Gwynn & Hadcock, *Medieval religious houses*, 174–5.   39 See above at p. 53.   40 Gwynn & Hadcock, *Medieval religious houses*, 188–9. Cf. Reeves, *Ecclesiastical antiquities*, 98.   41 The Collector, as Richard Sharpe (*Medieval Irish saints' Lives*) called him, responsible for the Marsh's Library version of Colmán's Life took the reference to be to the Lateran. Moreover, by quoting Matthew 11:11, he clearly understood the reference to be to John the Baptist, co-patron of the Lateran.   42 Lucius was a canon regular of San Frediano in Lucca, whose patron was taken to be of Irish origin by the author of his Life, the earliest copies of which date to the eleventh century; Tommasini, *Irish saints in Italy*, 365–6; Kenney, *Sources*, 184–5.

the Lateran to the Evangelist doubtless also came from Rome, but it is unlikely to have done so before the middle of the twelfth century, when travel from Ireland to Rome would have been quite common.[43]

The Salamancan Life locates the beginning of Colmán's career, his birth, upbringing, initial instruction, and early encounters with other saints in the north of Ireland, mostly in the area about Lough Neagh. Following his instruction by a saint named Caomhán, among others, he founded a little monastery (*monasteriolum*) with four monks, all of whom died of hunger (§3). Various miracles were then performed, including the resuscitation of a youth destined to become the saint known as Colmán Muilinn of Derrykeighan in north Antrim (§5). Three important northern boundary rivers are featured in successive passages of the text: the river Mion which separated Dál nAraidhe from Ceinéal Eoghain; the Bior, or Moyola, which served as a terminus of the diocese of Armagh, and the Dabhall, or Blackwater, which, like the Moyola, flows into Lough Neagh (§§8–10). This section of the Life concludes with an account, based on Adhamhnán's work, of the saint's passage to Iona (§13). Here, Colum Cille gave Colmán the gift of a cruet (*ampulla*) which, on being left behind, later turned up near the altar of Doire Calach (perhaps for Doire Calgach, now Derry), which was also to become the site of an Augustinian priory.[44]

The remainder of the Life is taken up with Colmán's activities in the Midlands, beginning with the above-mentioned story of the founding of Lynally which places the saint in Colum Cille's debt (§14). Like Colum Cille, Colmán is shown to have had the gift of second sight, illustrated here by his prior knowledge of the death of Pope Gregory long before the news otherwise reached Ireland (§20). His contacts with various other saints, such as Mochuda of Rahan whose church lay close to Lynally, and Molua of Clonfertmulloe who is cast in a deferential role, receive attention in the Life (§§25, 28, 50). The saint's visits to Ferns, Clonmacnoise, and Clonard, all of which later became locations of houses of canons regular, also receive mention (§§38, 40–1, 49–50). Moreover, as if to emphasize the closeness of Lynally's relationship with the church of Connor, Colmán foretells of its bishop, Díoma Dubh (†659), that he would provide all the churches of Ireland with succour and protection (§26). This prophecy arguably first became reality in the twelfth

---

43 St Malachy, for instance, is known to have twice embarked on a journey to Rome, accompanied by other clerics, in the ten years between 1138 and 1148, dying at Clairvaux while on his second journey. 44 Gwynn & Hadcock, *Medieval religious houses*, 168–9.

century in the person of Díoma's successor, Maol Maodhóg (Malachy) (§26), who occupied the primatial seat in Armagh. On the point of death, and surrounded by other saints, Colmán is said to have been allowed three petitions by the Lord, one of which was that, if wisdom were ever to be lacking on the island, a wise man would still be found in Lynally (§50).

Colmán's vernacular Life, a verse and prose composition, is largely concerned with the fortunes of local families that clearly had an interest in the church of Lynally. Included are the above-mentioned Muintear Chuinneagáin, the Uí Mhaomhuaidh lords of the surrounding territory of Fir Cheall, and their close relatives, the Uí Dhuineachaidh. At this point, relations with Durrow appear to have soured; monks of this church are accused of stealing 'Roman' earth from the burial ground in Lynally.

MANUSCRIPTS AND PREVIOUS EDITIONS

The Latin Life translated in this volume is preserved in the *Codex Salmanticensis*, now Bibliothéque Royale, Brussels, 7672–4, ff. 123ᵛ–9ᵛ, possibly an early fourteenth-century manuscript.[45] The most recent edition of this version of the Life is in Heist, *Vitae*, 209–24. Other Latin Lives of the saint are preserved in Marsh's Library, Dublin, Z.3.1.5 (formerly V.3.4), ff. 129ᵛ–32ᵛ and Trinity College Dublin 175, ff. 106 *sequitur*, and, albeit imperfectly, in the Bodleian Library, Oxford, manuscripts B 485 and B 505. The Marsh's Library version has been edited in Plummer, *Vitae*, i, 258–73. Up to now, none of the Latin Lives has been translated into English. A vernacular version of the saint's Life, almost entirely unrelated to the Latin versions, has survived in the hand of the early seventeenth-century Franciscan Mícheál Ó Cléirigh in Brussels, Bibliothèque Royale 2342–40. It has been edited and translated in Plummer, *Bethada*, i, 168–82; ii, 162–76. Full accounts of the manuscript transmission of the saint's various Lives can be found in Plummer, *Vitae*, I, lvii; idem, *Bethada*, I, xxxii–iii, and in Kenney, *Sources*, 399.

---

45 Ó Riain, '*Codex Salmanticensis*'.

The Life of Colmán of Lynally

Here begins the Life of abbot Colmán

1 ~ There was a man of the Uí Néill of admirable life called Colmán son of Beoghain, who received from the name of some wood the addition of Alo [Eala] to his own name. The parents of this Colmán fled with other crowds of subjects at a time of hostile devastation, and came to the valley of Oichle, where his mother's period of waiting to give birth was completed. When the hour to give birth had arrived, one of those assisting grasped the very dry wood of a carriage made of oak. She then placed the point of the piece of wood in the ground, upright against the root and, as is usual with women when giving birth, the mother held the piece of wood in her hands, and gave birth in that position. When she had delivered her holy son, the dry piece of wood she had held in her hand miraculously freshened and, now freshening, grew vigorously into a great tree, which remains visible to this day as a sign in memory of the boy chosen from out of his mother's womb.

2 ~ With God governing and dispensing, Colmán, still a young boy, was handed over by his parents to a holy man named Cainneach Caomhán, to be instructed by him in sacred doctrine and holy manners. Caomhán had some holy female working for him who, one day, while milking cows, was suddenly moved to anger against the boy Colmán who was helping her to tie the feet of the cows with spancels, and struck him with her left hand. When they had returned home, the elder Caomhán interrogated the woman, saying: 'Why did you harm the boy? Did you not see him helping you like a man, and yet not see God in his heart. Do you not know that you have offended God sitting in his holy sanctuary, together with his holy angels'. When she heard these words, the woman did penance with tears and wails and, when he saw this, the elder said to her: 'God has accepted your remorse but expect God's judgement. Tomorrow you will receive God's punishment'. On the following day, the left hand with which she struck the boy was torn off her body, and at once fell

to the ground. A heap of stones placed over the hand bears witness to it until the present day.

3 ~ When Colmán became an adolescent, he left his aforesaid master Caomhán to study the scriptures with other holy men. Then, when he had become steeped in holy scripture and disciplined in saintly conduct and standards, he set up a little monastery for himself. When built, Colmán happened to go to another place because of some need, leaving behind four monks, men accomplished in prayer and abstinence. Scarcity came upon them so that they spent many days without food, but their abbot had said when departing: 'See to it, brothers, that you do not go away from this place for any reason until I return'. He foresaw, namely, that their departure for heaven was imminent. They chose, therefore, rather to die of hunger than to transgress the word of their elder, and when three of them were dead and buried, the fourth, who was the youngest, was found alive by a swineherd. Taking pity on him, the swineherd said: 'Come brother with me and eat; I will carry you on my shoulders'. He replied: 'I shall not go because, soon, rest and refreshment without end will be given to me'. Once more the swineherd said: 'I shall go speedily and bring you food'. He replied: 'Brother, do not be vexed, it were far better for me to separate from my body and be with Christ for eternity. But remain on a little, so that you can bury me'. This the swineherd carried out. On the second day after his burial, Colmán returned and, seeing the fresh grave, dug at it. Then, while invoking the name of the Lord, he raised the youth from the dead. Responding to this, the youth declared: 'Father of mine, why did you make me return again in the flesh? I implore you to allow me eternal rest in the glory of God's kingdom'. The abbot said to him: 'Son of mine, remain with me just a little in body and you will once more find that joy'. The youth replied: 'Do not keep me, father, for it grieves me to be removed from the forever peaceful inhabitants for even one hour'. The abbot then questioned him: 'Do you know, son, of that sheet of gold of one ounce weight which I left with you'. He replied: 'I know of it, father; I placed it between the pages of this book'. The abbot then said to him: 'Go, son, and rest in eternal peace'. So he fell asleep, but, having raised the bodies of these brethren from their graves, Colmán carried them humbly on his own shoulders to another monastery.

4 ~ There was no water in that place, but, with much labour and danger, the brethren brought water from out of the deepest valleys, on their shoulders

along the slopes of various mountains. Taking pity on them, Colmán then pierced a rock with his staff and waters flowed, which supply the monastery up to the present day.

5 ~ Once, when Colmán heard the jubilant clamour of laymen, after they had killed a man, [he said]: 'Behold, I hear the voice of a son of life among these laymen, who will be a sheep of mine'. Colmán went over to the laymen to say: 'Let each of you speak to me so that I may know which of you will be Christ's sheep'. As they spoke, Colmán perceived the voice of an adolescent to whom he said: 'Son, you have been called by God, and you will join our brethren'. Their lord Tuadán replied: 'This one is my servant and I will not release him'. Colmán then said to the youth: 'Son, choose what you wish'. He replied: 'I shall follow thee, lord abbot, as far as I can'. At this, the holy man said that he should come to him but, being held back, the youth could not come in body to the holy man. However, now released from the flesh, his soul emerged, and he fell dead. When he perceived this, Tuadán was remorseful and said to Colmán: 'Abbot, I offer this youth and all of his to you, and pray for me and him'. When Colmán prayed for the youth, he rose from the dead, and became his companion until the end of his life; he was called Colmán Muilinn (of the mill), and he performed many miracles.

6 ~ A certain holy, very simple and innocent man was attached to Colmán but not constrained by the saint's rule. When fear of famine affected the brethren, he used to be sent to his own people, before frequently returning to the saint. At one time of hunger, he went off to visit his people and, finding them gathered in a place of assembly, spoke angrily to them, saying: 'Miserly people, why did you do away with the servants of God? Behold the man of God, Colmán son of Beoghain, and his brethren are dying of hunger near you, while you have food in duplicate in your homes. Already in these days two of the brethren have died of hunger'. When they heard these things, those people brought together in one place butter and curds and said to him: 'You know, father, that we cannot go to the church of holy Colmán, which is a long way away, but we will go with you to the borders of our region'. Giving thanks, he accepted this and they came with him to their furthest borders, before returning and leaving him there alone with their alms. Hoping in God only, as he had no help, either of men or horses, he sat down and slept and, waking without delay, he found himself lying at the gate of Colmán's church. Marvelling at this, he said: 'Lord, I wish this were not sleep'. Colmán, who

saw all this in his mind, said to the brethren to go to the brother sitting outside, who wished to console them. Going out, the brethren received him.

7 ~ On another day, a certain nobleman, accompanied by an adolescent, came to Colmán, who, gazing attentively, said: 'This adolescent will today die covered in his blood, but I nevertheless see him living to old age'. When he heard this, the nobleman became sad because he was very fond of the adolescent. As they were returning to their home, and halfway distant from the holy man, blood poured all over the body of the adolescent without the trace of any wound and, thus covered in blood, he died. His body was carried back to Colmán who, while praying, restored the dead boy to life. The boy then committed himself to serving the saint until death and, as the man of God had foretold, he died at a good old age.

8 ~ Once, there were two tribes at war about the river Main (Mion), the crueller and more wicked of which took all the river-boats that were there into their power, lest it prove possible for some holy man to come and restrain them. The other tribe, which was weaker and in great danger, asked Colmán to help, and he, obliged by force of necessity, walked dry shod across the river in view of the two peoples, without any boat. When they saw what was done, the hosts praised the Lord and did not resist the man of God, but made peace at his word.

9 ~ In the same way, but at another time, Colmán, having made the sign of the cross, walked dry shod across the river Moyola (Bior) in order to liberate a female captive from the servitude of some king.

10 ~ On another occasion, with Colmán wishing to find out whether he could free another maidservant in his usual manner, he arrived, seated in his carriage, at the river Blackwater (Dabhall), which happened to be in flood beyond its normal banks. As they hesitated, Colmán ordered his driver and all the brethren to enter the river. When they went in, they found no water in it, nor did the hooves of the horses become wet, for the water had solidified under the feet of the horses as if it were a stone pavement.

11 ~ Going on from there, they came in the evening to the monastic town of Aodhán son of Aonghas. On entering at the hour of vespers on Saturday evening, Colmán, looking around, saw another man cutting timber with an

iron axe, and he said to one of his followers: 'Tell this brother to rest; the day of the Lord is approaching'. Failing to consent at the first word, the man tried to strike another blow. At the word of the holy man, the axe became stuck in the timber and the man's hands were tied about the handle, and thus he stood, unable to move until Colmán prayed for him. He who had been foolish now offered himself to Colmán as a monk and served him until his death.

12 ~ On another occasion, Colmán came to the church of holy Lasair who, together with the sisters, had no food for the holy guests at their arrival other than a dish of meat. They killed, therefore, an animal and both holy men and women accepted its meat gratefully, except for two holy women who, instead of eating their share, concealed it in a closed vessel. On the following day, when they found two serpents in the closed vessel, they prostrated themselves at Lasair's feet and confessed their sin. Lasair replied: 'It is not I who will judge your fault but Colmán, whom you resisted; search for him, therefore, because, rising early, he went away today and whatever place in Ireland you will find him, he will judge you there'. Now, of the two, one was without sight, the other lame of foot, but they set out on their way immediately, the blind one carrying the vessel with the serpents in it, the lame one holding a stick in front of the other. When they had walked on their way, the one with sight saw a large gathering of people seated not far away. With the Lord taking pity on his maidservants, this turned out to be the coarb of the holy bishop Patrick and abbot of his monastery coming to meet Colmán Eala and, having sat down there, to greet one another. When they arrived, the two females passed through the crowds and lay flat at Colmán's feet, while confessing their sin in front of all with the words: 'Whatever you say to us, we will do it'. Colmán then said to them: 'It seems just to me that, by way of obedience, you now eat in front of the people the serpents you caused to grow by way of disobedience'. Straightway, they confidently took the vessel and made their way through the crowds in order to eat the serpents. Colmán then blessed the serpents with the sign of the cross and they turned into wheaten bread. When they ate the bread, the women were immediately free of their ailments, the blind one being able to see and the other able to walk firm of foot. All who witnessed this, praised the Lord.

13 ~ On another occasion, when Colmán set sail to go into exile, it transpired that he and his companions arrived at the Coire Breacáin (Whirlpool of Breacán). While praying, Colmán then blessed the sea and, at that hour on the island

of Iona, Colum Cille asked for prayers lest Colmán Eala be swallowed into the depths of the sea. By the grace of both, the brethren were saved and arrived on the island of Iona, where Colum Cille and his followers rejoiced greatly. When the guests had eaten, Colum said to Colmán: 'Do not bother about other peoples; do not leave behind your own Irish people; instead nourish them with the words of doctrine and grace that were given to you. For it was out of necessity that I came to this region, and I appeal earnestly to you to return home lest the country be drained of the word of God'. Accepting this advice, Colmán made preparations to return, while Colum Cille filled a cruet of oil for him at the altar, which he then [left behind]* when sailing joyously to Ireland. The next day, while praying at the altar in Doire Cal[g]ach, he saw in front of him the cruet he had left behind.

14 ~ After this, there was an assembly in the territory of the Uí Néill at which kings, namely Aodh Sláine, Aodh son of Ainmhire, and others were present, as were Colum Cille, Cainneach and Colmán Eala. Colum Cille then said to the kings: 'Give some land in your territory to Colmán so that he can found a monastery for God on it'. They replied that he could choose whatever place he wished. Aodh Sláine then said that there was another wood in the southern part of his kingdom, which might please Colmán if he were to see it. Colmán asked what its name was, and Aodh replied that it was Fiodh Eala. Colmán then said that his monastery and resurrection would be there. Thereupon Colmán and Laisréan, Colum Cille's steward, who was sent with him, went about the wood and selected the place in which Lynally was built. Colmán dwelt there with numerous monks, praying, fasting and discussing scriptural readings.

15 ~ It happened that there was great hunger among the brethren on the solemn feast of the Epiphany. Yet Colmán said to the cook that he should divide the food liberally among the brethren on that day. The cook responded that God might provide, to which the holy man added that if God did not do so, the cook should take measures of snow for butter. Colmán had scarcely uttered these words when they saw many men laden with alms they were bringing. They were carrying enough for almost a whole day for the many brethren until a certain, recently arrived and inexperienced brother said: 'Today, when people otherwise rest, we will not have any pause in our ministry'. Hearing

---

* As Heist (*Vitae*, 214n) suggests, the scribe has omitted here a word like *relinquens*.

this, Colmán said: 'If you had not spoken like this, brother, ministry of this kind would not be lacking from this place for as long as the island is inhabited. But because you spoke thus, this group of ministrants will rest now and forever'.

16 ~ A certain faithful and merciful man, Baodán by name, who belonged to the Ceinéal Cairbre, wished to bring alms to Colmán. Having gathered together the choicest foods, he filled up a carriage and attached oxen to it. The road he took was scarcely passable for men on foot and impassable for horse and oxen, even without carriages. Unaware of how it happened, the man was transported by God with wagon and oxen until he was to be seen at the monastery of the brethren.

17 ~ Some thieves from Munster came into the territory of the Uí Néill in order to plunder there. They made off with two cows used by Colmán for bringing wood to keep the fires going, but, as they prepared to kill the saint's animals, their hands and feet became rigid and stuck to the ground so that they could not move in any way. Others, who had not been aware of the crime, went to Colmán and told him what had happened. With Colmán praying for them, those thwarted laymen were freed.

18 ~ It happened on another day that the brethren had material for making beer, but the yeast was dead. Then the beer-brewer asked Colmán to bless the pot and, when he had done so, the liquor increased in the pot and flowed onto the ground. When he saw this, the brewer filled from the flow every vessel he had and, for as long as they could find vessels, the flow did not stop, and all of them were full.

19 ~ One of the monks among the brethren was a Briton who, for some cause of reproach, became angry with Colmán, so much so that he rose up to kill him. But, when he raised his hands to strike, he became immobile like a statue, with arms outstretched in the air, so that he could not move until he asked for forgiveness remorsefully and, with the holy man praying for him, he was released.

20 ~ One day, while out working with the brethren, Colmán suddenly prostrated himself on the ground in front of them, first weeping and lamenting and then, after a short interval, rising up and rejoicing with great happiness. The brethren then asked Colmán to indicate the cause of his sadness and happiness,

whereupon he said to them: 'Brothers of mine, I saw all the angels of God descending down to earth and, terrified with fear, I thought that the Day of Judgement had come and that is why I wept and lamented. Looking up again, however, I saw a golden altar being raised up in the hands of angels, and the soul of Pope Gregory of the city of Rome seated on the altar, and the earth was full of the light of the angels who sang sweet songs around the soul as far as heaven. That is why I was joyful and, when a year will have gone by from this day, a pilgrim will come to us from the city of Rome and announce to us that the soul of holy Gregory migrated to heaven on this day'. So it transpired, for a certain disciple of Gregory made a vow of pilgrimage to God, and questioned Colmán Dubhchuilinn with a view to finding out from him whom he should come to. Colmán said: 'Go to Colmán Eala for, had I not taken a vow of pilgrimage, I would come to him. I will give this witness of him because, if the school of the apostle John the Evangelist and that of Colmán Eala were in one place, I would not leave John for Colmán, nor Colmán for John, because they are equal for me'. That disciple came, moreover, from Rome to Colmán Eala at the end of the year and, as the saint had previously prophesied, he told of Gregory's death.

21 ~ While at work on a day in summer, the brethren were enduring perspiration and thirst, and some said among themselves: 'We carry out much hard work and inflict many tribulations on our bodies, and, despite the work we see, we do not know enough about what the future rewards will be'. This they said, not in a spirit of complaint or in hesitancy of faith but so as to receive consolation from their abbot Colmán who, hearing these things, said to them: 'Brothers, if you wish to witness the glory of the kingdom of God, you will now do so in as far as it is possible for mortals'. They replied: 'Yes, father, we do wish it, so that you will have consoled us'. Raising his hand, Colmán then blessed their eyes, which opened up and saw the glory of the heavenly kingdom in as much as they could bear to do so. Colmán commanded them not to tell this to any one during his lifetime, and they, full of the joy of the vision, were fervent of spirit and desirous of heaven for the rest of their days. They could scarcely be restrained by their abbot from valuing all present work highly because of the ineffable glory to come, some of which they had witnessed.

22 ~ Once, some poor people came to Colmán, seeking alms, but, as he had nothing to hand over to them, he gave a bronze vessel used to pour water on his head, with which they quickly departed. The man with care of guests and the poor

saw this, but the holy man's steward was not present. When he had returned, he went out, as was his habit, to bring water for the holy man's head and found the vessel in its usual place. He brought the water as was his wont in the vessel which God had given his saint. This vessel is still in Colmán's monastery today in witness of the miracle.

23 ~ Once Colmán was on a journey and, when he returned to his own place, he heard that one of his brethren, Collán by name, a very obedient man, had died the previous day. Throwing everything aside, Colmán went alone to the little cell in which the dead man lay and, standing at the door, said: 'Holy servant Collán, open this house for me and, just as you were obedient in life, be it also after death and open the door for me'. Although dead, Collán, quickly rising, opened up the house and, when they had greeted one another, he said: 'I beseech you to allow me return to God's kingdom, where I found great glory and repose in God's company'. Thus, having received the last rites, he was buried.

24 ~ At another time, when looking at his brother, a son of Beoghain, Colmán noticed that the lids of his eyes had been secretly painted the colour of hyacinth, as was the fashion. Since this was a great fault in the view of the holy man, he said to his brother that his eyes would have no sight during his lifetime. From that hour on until his death, he was blind.

25 ~ On a certain day, Mochuda came to the church of Molua of the Maca Oiche, with a single monk as companion. The companion said that he would like to stay with him, if the abbot allowed, and Molua agreed to it, since he so wished. Leaving early on his own, Mochuda placed two satchels full of books on his shoulders. When Molua's monks, who were working on the harvest, saw the old man walking alone, they smiled, saying: 'It's time for this old man to be in a monastery because it is undignified for old men to run about on their own'. But Molua said to them: 'Don't speak like that, for he whom you see walking alone today, his community of monks will one day be large by comparison with yours, and he will be abbot over many'. It happened namely that, as he walked on his way, two monks came to him and asked where he was going. He replied that he was going to Colmán Eala, and the monks asked him to receive them into his service, which he did. When they came to Colmán Eala, Mochuda said: 'Abbot, I wish to be one of your monks'. Colmán replied: 'You will be abbot of numerous monks and God did not

ordain for you to be a monk under the authority of another for, through you, many monks will serve God. Go, therefore, now to a nearby place called Rahan and stay there'. Carthach [alias Mochuda] then left with his two monks and, while frequently coming to Colmán to study, he built a church there.

26 ~ There were two boys in Colmán's monastery concerning whom he said to the steward and cook: 'Do not force these two to work, but keep them in food'. The steward and cook were thinking to themselves as to why the abbot had ordered freedom from work for these two boys in particular. Coming to Colmán, they lay flat in front of him and besought him to indicate the reason. He did this, saying: 'Rise up and I shall reveal what you wish to know but do not say it to any one during my lifetime. One of the boys is a son of hell and perdition and will live for a short time only, which is why he should not be kept in check under an ecclesiastical rule, because perpetual suffering is in store for him. The other boy is a son of life and the heavenly kingdom and he will live for a long time, holy and wise, a protector and helper of all the churches of Ireland. This is why he ought not to be killed by heavy work and niggardliness, because he will bring profit to many'. This one is Díoma Dubh.

27 ~ There came to Colmán a certain man by the name of Crónán who was possessed by a demon and, when this happened, he was accustomed to fall, often into fire and often into water. Colmán asked him whether he wished to have the demon leave him, and Crónán said that he did. Colmán then said: 'If you listen to me and do what I say, Satan will have no power over you, but you will have dominion over him'. Crónán replied that he would do everything he said to him. Colmán then declared: 'This is your cure; let the name of Jesus precede in your mouth every word you say throughout your life. If you keep doing that, Satan will not harm you and you'll receive the Holy Spirit'. Crónán kept doing it, and uttered nothing unless the name of Jesus accompanied every word. Through this, the Holy Spirit came down upon him so that he performed many miracles.

28 ~ One day, Mochuda came to Colmán and, when they had greeted one another, Colmán said: 'Let one of the boys with you run at once to where the brethren are milking the cows, because a crow is polluting the milk, lest one of the brothers be defiled in it'. On being sent by Mochuda, the boy found a shiny crow with a milky head.

29 ~ Some monks built a church for themselves at the confluence of two rivers but, when the rivers flooded after some time, their church was under threat. Those monks then came with the problem to Colmán who told them to take his staff and bless both themselves and the surrounds of their church with it. When they had done this, water did not harm them from that day until now.

30 ~ An evil man stole Colmán's cruet from its chrismal and, when an assembly of the churches heard about this, they apprehended the thief and led him to his death. Knowing this, Colmán went off to free him, but those at the assembly announced: 'We have sworn an oath that, unless he return the cruet, he will die'. Some cleric from the further reaches of Munster bought the cruet from the thief. Hearing this, Colmán lay flat on the ground in prayer and, before the prayer was finished, the cruet was to be seen, placed in front of all amidst the brethren. In this way, he freed the miserable man from death.

31 ~ A certain nobleman who had no offspring, his wife being barren, came to Colmán to appeal for help. Colmán said to him: 'Your wife will bear you a son whom you will call Ciarán; he'll be a monk of mine, long-lived and just'. The man responded by offering the boy to Colmán before he was born. On being born, Ciarán became a faithful, just and good man who came to Colmán on feastdays in order to receive the sacrament from his hands. When some evil and inimical men heard of this, they hid themselves on the way in order to kill him, but, when Ciarán and his lay companions were coming from afar, they saw the armed men, who then realized that this miracle was done by God through the merits of holy Colmán. Seeing this to be the case, they came to Colmán and did penance.

32 ~ On another day, Colmán came to the king, Aodh Sláine, to seek from him a man in captivity. At that hour, a ray of the sun shone from above through an opening in the roof of the summerhouse. When he saw the ray, the king said to Colmán: 'Just as you cannot make this ray of the sun stay in one place until evening, when the sun hurries towards sunset, so also you cannot obtain the freedom you seek for the captive'. The holy man replied: 'If I obtain from God a ray that stays, will you then release the captive to me?' The king responded: 'Why would I not give this man to you; for if you make the ray stay in one place until evening, you can take him against my will?' Invoking the name of the Lord Jesus, the saint then ordered the ray not to move. The ray remained in that one place until evening, while the sun quickly set. In this way, he had freed the captive by evening.

33 ~ On a day when the brethren were singing the hymn of St Patrick, Colmán saw Patrick standing in their midst. Colmán then sang the hymn three times, until an elder from among the brethren said: 'If we sing this one no further, we have some spiritual songs to hand'. Colmán then said: 'Behold, Patrick stood in our presence from the time we began to sing his hymn until he heard your words'.

34 ~ There was a certain nobleman of the Uí Néill, to whom a son was born, blind from the womb. The mother ordered one of her boys to kill the blind infant. But, as he was going with the child towards some swamp, the boy heard the voice of the infant speaking to him and asking whether he knew what task he was hurrying to do, to which he replied that he was going to kill him. The infant then responded, saying: 'Unless you do penance quickly, you will die and I shall be alive, for, since I have been given to Colmán Eala, you cannot kill me'. Becoming fearful, the boy returned home and recounted the infant's words to his father, who described it as an apparition and asked a female servant to carry the infant away to be killed. Truly, as she was going out with the infant, he spoke to her, saying that she could not complete the task, for he had been given to Colmán Eala and, unless she did penance, she would die. Returning, she repeated the infant's words, at which the father himself, rising up, carried away to his death the infant who spoke the same as before, saying: 'You shall die before you have completed the task you are going off to do, unless you do penance, for God has given me to Colmán Eala'. When he heard what the infant had to say, the father became very fearful and declared that he would not die because of the infant. At that time, Colmán was not far from the home of the infant and, coming there, he said to the father that it was an evil thing he had wanted to do, namely to kill the child. The father then gave the infant to Colmán, who baptized him and taught him wisdom and good behaviour so that he became a most learned teacher, full of grace; his name was Ceallán Caoch.

35 ~ One day, when Colmán was walking on his way, he came to some brethren for hospitality, but they had no butter in store for guests other than a little vessel belonging to some man, which had been deposited with them. This they gave to their guests and, with supper over, they confessed all this to Colmán. He then commanded that the traces of butter on the tables be placed in the original little vessel, which, on being blessed by him, again became full of butter, with another portion over and above.

36 ~ Some thief took a prey from the brethren in a place called Cluain Caoin. When he became aware of this in his mind, Colmán went to them and asked whether they knew who had taken their property. When they confessed not to know, he told them to come and he would lead them to where these were. They went off to the lands of the Laoighse and found them in Dún Salach but, when questioned on this matter, the thieves denied having done it, and were prepared to swear upon it at that hour. Colmán then said to them: 'We will leave you tonight and see what you do tomorrow'. That night, their arms swelled up and the twenty-five men were weighed down by great pain. In the morning, having confessed their sin, they did penance.

37 ~ Some day or other, when bread was being baked in the oven, a red-hot stone fell from the lit furnace. Holding it in his hand, Colmán threw the fire away from the furnace.

38 ~ On a certain day, Molua of the Maca Oiche came to Colmán Eala on some business and, after he had been entertained, the brethren wished to retain Molua for at least one day. Colmán said this to him, but he refused, saying that he needed to go that day. Colmán then commanded the brethren to seek from God what they had not obtained from man and, as Molua prepared to begin his journey, a great storm started, with thunder and lightning. Held back by God, Molua said to Colmán: 'I'll do the same to you; on a day when you are not willing, I'll hold you back'. So it transpired.

39 ~ On some other day, Brannabh, king of Leinster, who had become a friend of Aidan of Ferns by virtue of the many gifts he gave him, was killed. Aidan, who was truly sorry that he had accepted gifts of a king who then perished in an unforeseen way, fasted with his whole community for an entire year on bread and water. He also sent messengers to Colmán Eala, asking him to come but, not wishing to go this time, Colmán refused. Aidan again sent a message, asking him to come unless he wished to resist God. Heading off then, Colmán came to Clonfertmulloe, where he was entertained, and the holy men who were there pleaded with him to stay another day, but he did not wish to do so. As Colmán was beginning his journey at the very first light, fire happened to take hold of the monastery. All the brethren, together with the elders, rose at the sound of some clapping, and came towards Colmán who, raising his hand and blessing the fire, straightway extinguished it. With all the elders gathering about him with an unforeseen request, he then remained on.

40 ~ After this, when Colmán had arrived in Ferns, Aidan said: 'All year we've toiled, with fasts and prayers, on behalf of Brannamh's soul, but it appears that up to now he has earned no mercy, for his grave hardens, and produces no hay. Let you pray tonight, therefore, to see if some mercy might follow through you'. He carried this out, praying through the night and, when morning came, they saw that the grave had sprouted hay reaching the ankles. When he heard this, both Aidan and a holy Briton with him said to Colmán that the grave ought to be moved because Brannamh had received mercy through his prayer. They dug up the grave again and told Brannamh to rise up, which, after a year dead, he did, and the wounds of the body, which caused his death, were not to be seen. The Briton asked what the resuscitated man would do, and Aidan responded that he should return to his kingdom, where he had earlier been. The Briton then said: 'When he had the good fortune of a kingdom, this man lost sight of death, past and future, which, with others watching, will lead to inconstancy'. Aidan replied that it would be perhaps better if he again died.

41 ~ One day, when Colmán had come to Clonard, he found the brethren fasting because of some stolen linen garment, but they were joyous at his arrival. He said to them: 'If you wish to feed me, it will be a meal for all of us and I will give you tomorrow the garment you seek. The one who has the garment sought by you is among the brethren, and he will give it to me tonight. I will then give it to you and no one else will know about it, nor will the brother be embarrassed'. The brethren then said: 'We are fasting in vain, since the garment will be found tomorrow'. So it was done, as Colmán had said.

42 ~ Another day, Colmán was writing and, being full of the grace of the Holy Ghost, he copied the Psalter, the Acts of the Apostles and other books. Wise men say that as long as he could get vellum, the page was no sooner written than it dried, and this he did only towards evening. Someone once came to ask him about some unknown matter. He said to him: 'Do you want to make a prophet of me, like Colum Cille'. When he had said this, his talent for writing ceased.

43 ~ On a day when Colmán had come to Clonmacnoise, the brethren there asked him to preach the word of God to them. However, when he came to the gospel-book, he saw a demon next to the book, whereupon he said to the brethren: 'Pray for me; a demon is stuck to the gospel-book to keep me from

preaching'. The demon immediately fled and the sermon was such that they held that day at year's end in reverence for a long time, as if it were a feastday.

44 ~ A certain virgin by the name of Comna came to Colmán to ask that he come and free her people, because the king, Bréanainn son of Cairbre, was reducing them to servitude. On reaching her place, with a view to going with her to the king, they found his steward about to lead Comna's people to the king, together with their property. As Colmán and Comna walked along the way with them, they came to a large rock, which hindered all travellers. When he saw the hindrance, Colmán prayed that it no longer annoy people and, straightway, before the eyes of that crowd of people, the rock, flying lightly through the air, withdrew to another place. When he saw this miracle, the steward told the king about it but, when Colmán had come to the king and asked him to free Comna's people, he pitilessly refused to listen. God took the proud king immediately to task, however, so that he could neither see, nor hear nor speak. At this, the king, now humbled, did penance and freed the captive people, following which his eyes, ears and mouth were open. Colmán and Comna then returned.

45 ~ When they arrived, they found a little cell prepared at Comna's place but, as the attendants were carrying a vessel full of beer, they fell downwards and spilled it. On seeing this, and not wishing to have Comna upset, Colmán ordered the attendants to fill that vessel with water from the well. Straightway the water was changed into a good beer, for as long as guests of the holy man were consuming it, and enough beer was drawn from that well for them.

46~ Another day, as Colmán was on a journey in Connacht, he saw an attendance of angels in a certain place. When he had entered the place, to see what might be the reason, he found a rock frequented by angels. On inquiring as to what rock it was, he heard that [blood from] the head of a holy girl, who was killed with a sword – it being customary in those days to kill females – had trickled onto the rock. He ordered that the rock be brought to some church.

47 ~ It happened again in the province of Connacht that, while walking, Colmán left the direct road and did not know where he was going. He said to his companions: 'Let us sing the psalm that begins: "Blessed are the undefiled in the way". While singing this they found their way, and it led them to the home of a compassionate and hospitable man who received them with joy

and love. He said to them that all his relations had died of a plague then in progress and that he had no sons except the one they saw, who had neither eyes nor nostrils. In the morning, when the hospitality had ended and Colmán was praying in some place outside, the man said to him that it was a cause of great labour for him not to have water nearby. The holy man asked him to dig the ground and, when one sod was turned, a well of water rose out of the ground. As he was being thanked, the holy man told the man to bring his son and wash him in the water. When he had done so, Colmán blessed the boy who had neither eyes nor forehead nor eyebrows nor cheeks nor nostrils. With Colmán praying, the boy's natural healthy appearance was restored and his face was given shape.

48 ~ Another man came to him with his wife, bringing a deaf and dumb son and, when fetched, Colmán came. Sitting down with them, Colmán said to the deaf and dumb son: 'Kill the worms you see in my cloak'. Hearing this, the son responded, saying: 'I'll do what you command'. Thus cured, the son went off with his parents.

49 ~ When Colmán had a great desire to separate from his body and be with Christ, he travelled to Clonard, so that he might seek his request there, near the remains of holy bishop Finnian. Then, when in the guesthouse, with all asleep about him, he went to the church in which Finnian lay and, standing in front of the closed door, he said: 'Holy Finnian, open up your church to me'. Thus summoned, Finnian came and opened it for him, upon which Colmán said: 'I appeal to you to pray to the Lord on my behalf, so that I may go to him this year'. Finnian replied: 'God has received your prayer and you will depart this year for the kingdom of the Lord Jesus Christ'. When they had paid respects to one another, Colmán returned home joyfully.

50 ~ When the time of his departure from this world came, Colmán was given a sign from heaven in the form of a lighted cross which appeared in the sky. When they saw it, all the brethren were afraid of this unfamiliar miracle, but Colmán said to them: 'Do not fear, for this is a sign of my departure'. When the day of his death had arrived and he became ill, Mochuda of Rahan and other holy men from round about came to him. Colmán said to them: 'Be it known to you, my brethren, that these are the requests which the Lord has granted to me: whoever appeals to me at the hour of death will have life; whoever will have revered my feastday, will have mercy and, should wisdom

have failed on this island, a wise man will be found here'. When he had said this and similar things, he set free his soul and was buried.

51 ~ After Colmán's death, some thieves killed one of the monks who were serving the craftsmen doing building work on his church. When the corpse was brought, the brethren placed Colmán's staff on it and the dead man rose up, alive and well.

52 ~ After some time, Colmán appeared in a vision and ordered that his bones be elevated from his grave in the ground, lest they be stolen from there. Then all the brethren, together with people from the surrounding area, elevated his remains and, while praising and blessing the Lord, who has everlasting honour and glory, with psalms, hymns and spiritual canticles, they placed them with great honour in an ornate shrine. Amen.

The Life of Fíonán of Kinnitty

THE SAINT

Fíonán's principal church was located at Kinnitty in Co. Offaly. However, his pedigree attached him to the Corca Dhuibhne, whose eponymous ancestor, Corc Duibhne, is described as a son of Cairbre Músc, eponymous ancestor of the Múscraighe, alias Síol Conaire.[1] The Corca Dhuibhne gave name to the barony of Corkaguiny in west Kerry but they also formerly controlled the Iveragh peninsula, where there were most dedications to the saint.[2] Fíonán was regarded as one of the chief protectors of the Corca Dhuibhne and as one of three *coinnle*, 'candles', of the Múscraighe, the others being Laichtín of Donaghmore and Seanán of Scattery Island.[3] Fíonán's father, here named Mac Airdhe (§1), is called Maonach mac Airdhe (Ardha) in the saint's pedigree. Nothing else is recorded of Maonach but Mac Airdhe son of Fiodhach was regarded as king of Ciarraighe Luachra, a territory comprising most of east Kerry.[4] Moreover, Mac Airdhe is said to have been a uterine brother of Ciarán of Clonmacnoise who is not mentioned in Fíonán's Life.[5] Of Fíonán's mother, whose father is variously named Cian and [F]iodhgha, little else is known, other than her attachment to the Ciarraighe Luachra.[6] In one account of the saint's conception (§1), his mother is said to have been bathing at the time in Killarney Lower Lake, which would place the event near the church later dedicated to the saint on Inisfallen.[7]

In early notices of his feast, Fíonán is attached to the Midlands church of Kinnitty but, from the twelfth century onwards, accounts of the saint and his activities give equal or even more space to his *patria* in south Kerry. For example, the late twelfth-century Martyrology of Gorman assigns him to both Kinnitty and Inisfallen, and his biographers devote more space to his activities in Kerry

---

1 *CGSH* §211. 2 The priest-poet, Seán Ó Conaill, a native of south Kerry, who appealed for aid to a saint named Fíonán in his well-known *Tuireamh na hÉireann*, 'elegy of Ireland', assigned 'his saint … who saved Iveragh from the plague', to both Inisfallen on Lower Lake, Killarney, and to Waterville Lake (O'Rahilly, *Five seventeenth-century political poems*, 81). 3 *CGSH* §665.7. 4 Meyer, 'Laud genealogies', 315; *HDGP* iv, 145. 5 Meyer, 'Laud genealogies', 315; *CGSH* §722.16.57. 6 *CGSH* §722.81; *MartO* 112. 7 *MartO* 112.

75

than to his time in the Midlands. For its part, the saint's feastday is the subject of some confusion. In south Kerry it falls on 16 March, the day assigned by the martyrologies to a namesake, Fíonán Lobhar, 'leprous Fíonán', of Swords, whereas 7 April appears to have been the day observed in Kinnitty.[8] If he was also patron of Killinane (Ceall Fhíonáin?), near Cahersiveen, as seems likely, he was commemorated there on 3 March, and patterns were held at a well dedicated to him near Kenmare on 3 May and 14 September.[9] The cult also spread out from Kinnity, for example, to Rearymore in Laois, where a holy well preserved his memory.[10] The saint's rib is said to have formed part of Adhamhnán's reliquary, and his grave (*Leacht Fhíonáin*) was reputedly located on a hill in the Kerry parish of Killinane.[11]

The saint is scarcely noticed in Lives other than his own, an exception being that of Bréanainn, which gives Fíonán the privilege of being the only one who could look at his face, such was its abundance of grace.[12] Although otherwise not said to have travelled outside Ireland, Fíonán is nonetheless credited with having brought wheat into the country.[13] A poem attributed to Moling of St Mullin's in Carlow shows Fíonán blessing a family of the Ciarraighe named Clann Aingeadha.[14]

THE CHURCH

Being a relatively minor church, Kinnity is rarely mentioned in either annals or the wider literature.[15] The church stood on the grounds now occupied by the Church of Ireland building, whose porch contains an early Christian decorated graveslab.[16] Two ninth-century abbots are recorded, together with an early tenth-century abbot who was slain at the battle of Ballaghmoon in Co. Kildare in 909, on the side of the men of Munster against the Leinstermen. Significantly, his name is followed in the list by that of the king of Corca Dhuibhne, which may mean that his church was already in that period closely associated with south Kerry.[17] A final mention of a coarb of Fíonán occurs in the Annals of Inisfallen with the death in 1033 of a man named Cathal

8 *MartG* 56, 72. The March feast assigned to Fíonán of Swords in Co. Dublin was the present saint's day in south Kerry (*DIS* 329).   9 O'Donovan, *The antiquities*, 145, 233; Seabhac, *Uí Ráthach*, 49.   10 Herity, *Ordnance Survey letters Laois*, i, 204.   11 Carney, 'A maccucáin', 34 §11; Seabhac, *Uí Ráthach*, 51. 12 Plummer, *Vitae*, i, 100–1 §5; Heist, *Vitae*, 326 §4.   13 *MartO* 112.   14 *Anecd.* 32 §15; O'Brien, *Corpus*, 161a11.   15 *HDGP* iv, 76–7.   16 *AICO* §681; Fitzpatrick & O'Brien, *Medieval churches*, 5. 17 *AFM* s.a. 850, 884, 903.

9. Present Church of Ireland church in Kinnitty on the site of the early Christian church, courtesy of Stephen Callaghan.

Béarlaidh, 'Cathal the Linguist'.[18] However, this may well refer to an abbot of the saint's church on Inisfallen, which gave name to the annals. It is thought that the Kinnitty High Cross, now in the grounds of Kinnitty Castle hotel, was brought there from the more important church of Drumcullen.[19]

18 *AI* s.a.   19 O'Brien, *Stories*, 141, 204.

THE LIFE

The author of the saint's Life was mainly concerned with the saint's activities in south Kerry, in the areas about Lower Lake (Loch Léin), Killarney, and Waterville Lake (Loch Luighdheach) near the Iveragh coast. The saint is said to have been born of a noble family in Corca Dhuibhne, and to have been educated by Bréanainn of Ardfert and Clonfert (§§1, 4). Bréanainn is also said to have directed Fíonán to the place of his resurrection at Kinnitty, but almost immediately afterwards the saint was brought back to Kerry, where he arranged for the miraculous transfer of a boat from Killarney to Waterville (§§9, 11). Then, having returned to the Midlands for one episode, he was again in his 'own country' performing many miracles, including the relief of a threat posed by Neachtan, king of Uí Fhidhgheinte, an area corresponding roughly to the present extent of the diocese of Limerick (§21). Back in Kinnitty once more, Fíonán taught manners to a Munster king named Fáilbhe Flann, before blessing him, and almost immediately showed favour to a man named Carthach, providing him with a single shoe, a symbol associated with sovereignty (§§26–7). In the remainder of the Life, the saint is shown to have had dealings with the Ciarraighe of north Kerry and the Eoghanacht of Raithleann in Cork, as well as associations with two persons in south Kerry, Mocheallóg, probably of Kilmakillogue (Ceall Muicheallóg) in the parish of Tuosist, and an unnamed craftsman in Waterville (§§30–2, 35). The saint's death is then described, without any mention of where it occurred (§37).

The fact that the saint's Life allows him to spend most of his time in Kerry scarcely favours a Kinnitty provenance. The focus of the text on Killarney's Lower Lake and Waterville Lake reflects the positions of churches that formed part of the spread of devotion to Fíonán who, as already stated, was patron of Inisfallen and of several places in the Waterville area, including the church of Killemlagh.[20] These associations are increasingly attested in documents dating from the late twelfth century, by which time Augustinian canons had established a priory on Inisfallen, followed by a second foundation in the parish of Prior, near Waterville, of which Fíonán was also patron.[21] The fact that the latter priory was dedicated to St Michael, and otherwise known as *De rupe Michaelis*, shows that it catered to pilgrims to Skellig Michael. Known to have had a scriptorium, at the latest by the middle of the twelfth century,

---

20 De Brún, 'Kerry diocese in 1890', 148.   21 Ibid.; Gwynn & Hadcock, *Medieval religious houses*, 180, 192.

Acta Sancti Finani.

Incipit Vita Sancti Finani.

Finani genus.

1. Finanus sanctus de genere Cor-
coduibne ortus fuit: et nomen patris
ejus Mac Airde, mater vero ejus
vocabatur Becnait. Conceptio autem
illius ita facta [1] est. Vidit enim mater ejus piscem de auro rubicundo
volantem ab ortu solis, et quod in-

Sanctitas ejus prodigio

travit per os ejus in ventrem, et de
illo concepit. Et hoc indicavit viro
sapienti et religioso ; qui dixit ei :
*Conceptus tuus sanctus erit et habebit
gratiam Dei.*

quod sepes non erat inter illos. Tunc
Finanus et traxit [3] baculum suum
post se per terram, et non aussus
est unus eorum transire vestigium
baculi sancti, sed lambebant vacce
vitulos suos trans vestigium.

4. DIXIT autem sanctus Branda-
nus Mac Cualte ad parentes ejus:
*Magnus erit filius vester coram Do-
mino.* Deinde venit ad Brandanum,
ut legeret et disceret regulam cum
eo. Fiebat [4] autem apud Brandanum contra fornacem vij annis [5].

vestigio baculi ejus accessiti.

Versatur sub disciplina S. Brandani Mac Cualte.

10. Opening passage of the first modern edition of Fíonán's Life in C. de Smedt & J. de Backer, *Acta sanctorum Hiberniae ex codice Salmanticensi nunc primum integer edita* (Edinburgh & London, 1887), col. 305.

Inisfallen would have been a likely place of composition for the Life.[22] An Augustinian connection may also explain the choice of Fíonán's mentor, Bréanainn. He was patron, not only of Ardfert in Co. Kerry, but also of Clonfert, the seat of a house of canons, founded possibly as early as the 1140s, and located a mere fifteen miles or so from Kinnitty.[23]

The politics underlying the Life can also be explained by reference to twelfth-century developments in west Munster.[24] Three of the kings that received favours from the saint – Feidhlimidh, Fáilbhe Flann, and Carthach – appear in the same order in the pedigree of the powerful Mac Carthaigh (MacCarthy) family, which first came to prominence in south Munster about 1100.[25] During the 1120s, Cormac, a prominent member of this family, was involved with Toirdhealbhach Ua Conchobhair of Connacht in a prolonged struggle for supremacy, which involved numerous other Munster families, including those of south Kerry. In 1124, Muircheartach Ua Muircheartaigh, king of the Eoghanacht of Lough Leane, was banished by Cormac to Connacht, returning in the following year to raid Corca Dhuibhne and the Killarney area with the aid of a fleet of boats.[26] This series of incidents may underlie the episode in

22 Mac Airt, *Annals of Inisfallen*, xxix–xxx.   23 Gwynn & Hadcock, *Medieval religious houses*, 164–5.
24 Ó Riain, 'Fíonán of Iveragh'; *DIS* 329.   25 Ó Murchadha, *Family names*, 49–50.   26 *AI s.a.*

Fíonán's Life that describes how the saint saved Corca Dhuibhne from invasion at the hands of a king of the Uí Fhidhgheinte named Neachtan, whom one source describes as an ancestor of Muircheartach Ua Muircheartaigh.[27]

On the foregoing evidence, therefore, Fíonán's Latin Life is likely to have been first written down in the mid- to late twelfth century. Later Lives of the saint pursued their own agenda. The latest of them, a vernacular Life surviving in at least eight manuscripts, may have been written at 'Killagh Abbey' in the Kerry parish of Kilcolman, near Milltown, which Abán, having foretold Fíonán's birth, is elsewhere said to have bestowed upon the saint.[28]

MANUSCRIPTS AND PREVIOUS EDITIONS

Fíonán was made the subject of several written Lives, the earliest being that of the Salamancan codex (*codex Salmanticensis*) which was arguably compiled in a house of canons regular of St Augustine at Clogher in Tyrone in the early fourteenth century. This version of the Life, here abbreviated S, was most recently edited by W.W. Heist.[29] The S version was followed by two other recensions, one of which, in the Kilkenny codex (*codex Kilkenniensis*), and here abbreviated M, is kept in Marsh's Library, Dublin. It is among the Latin Lives edited by Charles Plummer.[30] The other Latin version, still unpublished and here abbreviated R, is preserved in two Rawlinson manuscripts, numbered 485 and 505, in the Bodleian Library, Oxford.[31] Fíonán was also made the subject of a vernacular Life preserved in two early seventeenth-century manuscripts, one of which, Royal Irish Academy, Dublin, A iv 1, here abbreviated as Stowe, has been edited without translation by 'Fáinne Fionn'.[32] The other, Brussels, Bibliothèque Royale, 2324–40, folios 135–8, has yet to be edited. A later vernacular version, which survives in some manuscripts, has been edited with translation by R.A.S. Macalister.[33] As Macalister pointed out, the lexicographer Edward O'Reilly cited forms from a vellum copy of this version of the Life.[34] Unlike the earlier version, this is closer to S and R than to MT, and closest to R, a copy of which appears to have been its source.[35] The S text, which most closely represents the source of all versions of Fíonán's Life, is here translated.

---

27 O'Brien, *Corpus*, 329a39.   28 Macalister, 'Life of Saint Finan'; Plummer, *Bethada*, i, 8 §24; idem, *Vitae*, i, 17 §22.   29 Heist, *Vitae*, 153–60; Ó Riain, 'Codex Salmanticensis', 91–100.   30 Plummer, *Vitae*, i, llxvii–lxx; ibid., ii, 87–95.   31 Ibid., llxvii–lxx.   32 Fáinne Fionn, 'Beatha Fionáin'.   33 Macalister, 'Life of Saint Finan'.   34 Ibid., 548.   35 Plummer, *Miscellanea*, 189. See notes to §§11, 12, 15.

The Life of Fíonán of Kinnitty

THE LIFE OF HOLY FÍONÁN, ABBOT OF KINNITTY

The Life of Fíonán, abbot and confessor, begins.

1 ~ Holy Fíonán belonged to the family of Corca Dhuibhne; his father's name was Mac Airdhe and his mother was called Beagnaid. This is how he was conceived; his mother saw a fish of reddish colour airborne from the direction of the rising sun, which entered her womb through her mouth, and she conceived from it. She told this to a wise and religious man who said to her: 'The child in your womb will be a holy man, and he will have grace from God'.

2 ~ Wherever his mother went, for as long as he was in her womb, not a drop of rain, snow or hail touched her garment; her spittle cured every illness and feebleness, and whatever she served of food, however little or poor, it was enough for one and all. When he was a boy, whenever one of the other small boys playing with him had a pain it was immediately cured. He used also foretell what was in store for each one of them, and so it used to turn out.

3 ~ Another time in summer, he was sent to mind some calves, which, while he was reading nearby, ran off to the cows, there being no fence between them. Fíonán then dragged his staff after him along the ground, and not one of them dared to cross over the mark of the holy boy's staff, but the cows licked their calves across it.

4 ~ Bréanainn of the Maca Alta said to the parents that their son would be great before God. Afterwards, he came to Bréanainn to read and learn the monastic rule with him, which he did for seven years over the oven.

5 ~ On another day, he brought with him from the wood the makings of a staff without the permission of his abbot Bréanainn who, when he noticed, threw the timber into the furnace. Not only did the fire not burn the timber, it shaped it in the form of a staff, as Fíonán had wished.

6 ~ Another day, some bread fell from him into the fire, at which Bréanainn said: 'Fíonán, the fire will burn your bread'. However, Fíonán was then preoccupied with something else, and did not draw the bread straightway out of the fire. After a while, however, he put his hand into the middle of the fire for the bread and neither hand nor bread was affected.

7 ~ On a certain day, one of the brethren, who was ill and near death, requested of Fíonán that he come out and give him the Eucharist. Fíonán said to the messenger: 'I cannot come until enough bread is made to satisfy the brethren but, in God's name, tell the soul not to leave the body until I come'. So it transpired; the soul remained in the body from early morning until he arrived in the afternoon.

8 ~ Another day, when they saw that the bread-hut was on fire, the brethren ran to extinguish it, until Bréanainn said: 'Wait, brethren; the fire you see is the grace of holy Fíonán'. They then saw Fíonán sitting inside the house on his own.

9 ~ At that, Bréanainn said to Fíonán: 'It does not behove us to remain in one place, so if it pleases you, remain here among the monks, and I shall go away'. Fíonán replied: 'Bless me for I am junior to you; where shall I go'. 'Go', said Bréanainn, 'to the mountain of Sinór, where you will find a herd of wild pigs, and stay there'. He then left, found it accordingly, and stayed on in the place called Kinnitty.

10 ~ Nine laymen came to Fíonán on a certain day, looking for some food to eat. As he was at the time offering up a mass, the official said to them: 'Wait a little until the elder will have received the host'. However, they all said that they needed to hurry. The official left and told this to the elder, who said: 'Give them whatever you have'. After these words, alms was brought to him by a holy woman, namely nine loaves of bread and their measures of butter, and each was given his portion, namely a loaf and its measure. They then battered one another with the butter, at which the official said: 'The devil taught you to do this evil thing'. They then slashed his face, and he fled into the church to his elder. At this, Fíonán said to them: 'You will all be killed today before sunset and, from this day until the Day of Judgement, any layman who will eat our butter will be killed before he will have digested it'. What he said to them was fulfilled before sunset. However, two men who forbade

the evil they were doing escaped back to Fíonán and he protected them. From that day on, no layman dares to eat that place's butter.

11 ~ On another occasion, a raft was made on the island on which Fíonán was staying, and he sent a message to the king of Loch Léin, Feidhlimidh by name, to come and carry it away with him. The king came to him with three hundred men but they could not carry the raft. Afterwards, angels of God came with Fíonán and carried the raft over Loch Luighdheach.

12 ~ At a certain time, when Fíonán was walking on a road, some laymen wished to strip and kill him, together with his companions. Behold! Another armed man, Lonán son of Finneach by name, came to the holy man's assistance and did not allow the others to harm him. Fíonán then said to Lonán: 'Whatever battle you take part in until the day of your death, you will not be overcome by your enemies'.

13 ~ On one occasion, when most blessed Fíonán went off to his native place in the lands of the Munstermen, he came for hospitality to Mac Gairbhe's place. A holy man who loved God, Mac Gairbhe slew a calf of the only cow he had when Fíonán arrived. On the following day, knowing that Mac Gairbhe had slain his only calf for the guests, Fíonán pleaded with God, and a beautiful calf came from on high in its place.

14 ~ Fíonán's horse died in Mac Gairbhe's place, but Jesus quickly sent a handsome, hyacinth-coloured horse with a white head, which, on coming to the holy man from out of Loch Léin, took the place of the earlier horse for three years, meekly and tamely. When it had travelled the lands of the Munstermen under Fíonán's carriage for three years, the saint ordered it to return once more to Loch Léin, and it departed at Fíonán's command.

15 ~ On some other day, when Fíonán was travelling in his wagon, he discovered a large leafy tree lying fallen across the road. Fíonán said to it: 'Rise so that the wagon can pass by on a clear road'. It straightway did so and, after Fíonán had passed by, it leaned down once more as before, and not even a single branch of the tree was broken.

16 ~ On some festive day, when Fíonán was at the boundary of Corca Dhuibhne, at Ráith Maca Lapa, the people asked if they might go to watch games. Fíonán

said: 'Let your bodies stay here near me, and let your souls depart'. It was done as he said; as they slept near the saint, their souls left for a faraway lake, where they saw the games, with a king seated in a beautiful place of assembly. When the souls returned to their bodies before evening, they related all that had been done at the games, just as they were.

17 ~ On another day, when Fíonán was travelling in his carriage, he came across a wet marsh surrounded by a narrow estuary of the sea, which he could not avoid. He then ordered his driver to direct his carriage through the marsh surrounded by the sea. He did as told and they crossed over marsh and estuary as if they were on a clear and dry plain, and neither a nail of the horses nor a wheel of the wagon became wet.

18 ~ On some day or other, a small, paralytic boy, who could move neither hands nor feet nor any limbs, was brought to him. Fíonán touched with his hand all the boy's bones, and said to him: 'Rise up in the name of Jesus Christ, see the sun and walk'. He straightway rose up.

19 ~ While Fíonán was living on some island, his horses, which were in a field beyond the lake, swam over to him on their own, with their legs tied together. They then went to his house without anyone leading them. When they had seen him, and he had blessed them, they swam back again to their field.

20 ~ When Fíonán was at Ráith Maca Lapa, he became thirsty and asked the steward for water. With the steward excusing himself because the water was far away, Fíonán told him to turn the sod near him. On this being turned, a well of the purest water flowed out.

21 ~ Once, when the Corca Dhuibhne were in distress for fear of troops of soldiers of the Uí Fhidhgheinte who wanted to ravage and kill them, they asked Fíonán for help. Fíonán went off to plead with the king, who was called Neachtan, but he, not wishing to greet him, sent a messenger out to meet him. Fíonán met up with the messenger in the hope of making a one-month truce, but [the king] said: 'I will not make one and, when I come, I shall plunder and destroy them'. Fíonán returned to his own people and consecrated water for them to drink against the cursing, and told them to wait in their own territory and not to cross over their borders and, if they were to overcome their enemies, not to glorify or exalt themselves, or howl in triumph. Then, when the enemy

came, five thousand were overcome by a mere two hundred, with God helping Fíonán, and thirty men of the enemy fell. Fíonán then once more went to plead with the king who still would not listen to him, and the more he pleaded, the more the king was excited to fury. Again, Neachtan's army was defeated and thirty of his men fell in every single battle, but the king remained obdurate. Going out to meet the king's messenger, Fíonán said to him: 'The horse of Neachtan son of Ceannfhada will die today and, if this prove to be the case, by this hour tomorrow he will no longer be king because his kingdom and ordination will be removed from him. He will be an exile for seven years and, when the exile is completed, he will be obliged to bring timber from the woods on his shoulders, even if he does not wish to do so. Though now surrounded by delights and feathers in good dwellings, all that will then remain for him will be the opportunity of finding a hollow piece of timber in the wood where he can rest his head, and his need will be served by a small piece of the meat of some lean animal which wolves eat. Because he is disobedient to me today, he will not have the kingship again until all these things are completed, and until he spends time with me in service winnowing chaff from grain. He will not be king until he has come to love with devoted heart the race which he now persecutes'. When Fíonán had said this, king Neachtan's army saw fire consuming the houses of their province, and the camps of the king being entirely destroyed by the same fire. Terrified by this, each and every one of them took to flight as if their homes had been entirely consumed. After they came back to the houses they had previously seen certainly on fire, they found them nonetheless intact with not even their furthest thatch burned, and all of this was done so that they would fear Fíonán. Everything he prophesied of the king came to be; his horse died and he became an exile for seven years, going to Diarmuid, king of the Uí Néill, whose steward told him to carry loads of timber on his shoulder to the fire, which he did. Afterwards, leaving king Diarmuid behind, he wandered around with five men and found nothing to protect him from rain and hail but the hollow timber of some leafy tree. When his family went looking for food, they found a red animal that was being devoured by wolves, part of which he ate. After all this, he went and served Fíonán and later, helped by the holy man, he again held the kingship.

22 ~ Some man came to Fíonán with a complaint, saying: 'What shall I do; I still have a long way to go, and I wish to go as quickly as possible, because I need to hurry'. Fíonán took pity on him and blessed him so that the man walked in three hours what another would scarcely do in three days.

23 ~ Another time, Fíonán's brother came to Kinnitty from his home territory in Corca Dhuibhne. His brother was in anguish, and complained to Fíonán that strangers were to come into his inheritance unless he provide the equivalent of seven female servants on a certain day. Fíonán was not very concerned about this until the day in question arrived, when his brother needed to provide the equivalent of seven female servants. At this point, aware that the time to hand them over on the following day was fast approaching, his brother, who came from afar, again complained. On the following night, preceding the due date for the handing over, his brother was taken away while asleep, without his noticing, and woke early in the morning to find himself in his own home in Corca Dhuibhne. There he saw the equivalent of seven female servants, which he handed over at the due time in restoration of his inheritance.

24 ~ Another day, when Fíonán's community were reaping a harvest, there was a great fall of rain. When Fíonán saw this, he pleaded with the Lord so that not a drop touched his harvesters from morning to evening. Not a drop fell on their field, even though it rained on all sides of where they were. This was a miracle because Fíonán's wagon was against the outside fence of the field, with its front part and yoke across the fence, where it remained dry, while the body of the wagon, which was outside the fence, became wet.

25 ~ On a certain day, as Fíonán was out walking, he happened to meet up with a captive being led off to be killed. He requested that the captive be handed over to him but did not obtain this. When the captive's enemies had raised their hands to kill him, they could not use them. The captive was then released to Fíonán.

26 ~ Another day, when Fíonán went to Treadhua of the Kings, where Fáilbhe Flann was, he asked the king to remit a tax on his people. At this, the official of the king swore at Fíonán, saying: 'Even if you were to fast for seven days, the tax would not be revoked'. The saint then said: 'If you will not let go the tax for me, the house you live in will be consumed by fire'. This is what happened, for in the blink of an eye fire came from heaven and devoured the dwelling, while, at the same time, the official was made mute. Fíonán performed a twin miracle in the presence of the king; he freed the tongue of a dumb boy brought to him, while binding the tongue of the loquacious official whom he struck dumb. King Fáilbhe then did penance and remitted the tax, for which the saint blessed him, and his official was healed.

27 ~ Fíonán also cured another man, by the name of Carthach who, while suffering from severe pain and lack of sleep for a year and a half, could not be cured by the doctors. After Fíonán blessed him, he slept for three days and nights and, though cured, pain remained in his foot so that he would fear God always. Fíonán made a sandal for him and said to him: 'If it were to be about your foot every day, it would not fail all your life, but know this; on the day you cannot go out with the sandal about your foot, pray to God, for the day of your death will be approaching'. It turned out as Fíonán had foretold.

28 ~ In some place or other, the foot of Fíonán's horse fractured under the cart, but, within that same hour, the holy man, having made a blessing with the sign of the cross, healed the foot and joined the bones together. At this, the horse climbed the mountain under its yoke without any difficulty.

29 ~ On another occasion, Fíonán asked a king to free a hostage but the king's son was unwilling to do so, upon which he was immediately struck dumb. Fíonán then said to the king: 'If you were to release the hostage to me, your son would be well again'. That is what happened.

30 ~ One of Fíonán's monks became infirm and could not walk for a full year until Fíonán, visiting him on a certain day, blessed him, saying: 'Rise up and you will come with us to the region of Ciarraighe Luachra and hold our horses for us'. So it was done; he who was infirm crossed Sliabh Luachra with them neither on horseback nor in a cart, but on foot.

31 ~ On some other day, when Fíonán was at games in Raithleann, there was a great fall of rain, which wet all clothes, but not a drop fell on Fíonán's garment. All who witnessed this praised God and Fíonán.

32 ~ On another occasion, Fíonán came to a religious man named Mocheallóg who dwelt in a place where he had two cows and one calf, as the calf of the other cow had been devoured by wolves. Since the one calf was loved by the two cows, Mocheallóg said that it be led from the field into the fort, lest it be eaten by wolves. When one of Fíonán's companions heard this, he said: 'For as long as Fíonán will be in this place your calf will not perish'. Nonetheless, a wolf came that night and devoured the calf. When his driver told Fíonán that wolves had devoured Mocheallóg's calf, he went out to the church and prayed, after which he said to Mocheallóg: 'Go and milk your

cows'. When he had gone off to the byre, the guilty wolf came in place of the calf, humbly and apologetically, and stood tamely in front of the cows, which licked it as if it were their calf. When Fíonán had become aware of this, he said: 'What the wolf did will not be enough, because it is unnatural for a wolf to stand around like a calf in the presence of cows, so let it go and search for a calf in place of the one it devoured'. The day after it had gone off to search, the wolf returned accompanied by a white, red-eared calf, which remained with the cows until they became feeble. Fíonán then said to Mocheallóg: 'Once your cows will have become feeble, the white calf will no longer remain with you, but this wolf will be the guardian of your calves, just like a well-behaved dog, until it dies, and will not harm any living soul'. So it turned out.

33 ~ When Fíonán had been sitting in some place of assembly, a woman gave him the head of an onion to bless because she was in pain. When Fíonán could not bless it immediately because of the business of the assembly, the woman nevertheless took the head away with her, unblessed but consecrated because it had been in his hand. Fíonán then said to the woman: 'Because of your faith, this pain that now troubles you will not do so until the day of your death'. So it was.

34 ~ Fíonán cured five paralytics and five dumb people at the cross standing at the entrance to his church.

35 ~ In a place near Lough Currane, where Fíonán had arrived for a function, the smith's pincers broke as he reached the place. The smith asked him what he should do and Fíonán told him to hold the metal in his hands. The smith then took hold of the hot metal and held it in his hands until the implement was made whole again.

36 ~ On another day, Fíonán sent one of his servants to catch fish in a field where cows were grazing, even though there was no water in the field, only dry earth. Fíonán said to his servant: 'Behold! Guests will be coming to us today, so go to the field and catch three fish for us in expectation of the guests'. The servant then went off without hesitation at the word of his elder and brought back three fish from the waterless field, as Fíonán had said.

37 ~ When the day of his death had come closer, his whole body became infirm. 'Now', he said, 'it is time for me to leave my body, but I shall not die until a

certain sick woman, who is being brought to me on a couch from afar, will arrive'. When she had been brought to him, she straightway returned healed to her own home. Afterwards, angels of God came towards him from heaven, with choirs and canticles and divine songs, to carry him to God's place of judgement, where he shines like the sun in God's kingdom forever and ever. Amen.

Notes to the Lives

THE LIFE OF CIARÁN OF CLONMACNOISE

§1   The vernacular Life opens with a homily (*LisL* ll. 3916–81; cf. *MartO* 204) which includes the claim that Ciarán's birth was prophesied by the three 'national' saints, Patrick at Croagh Patrick, Brighid at a place called Crosa Brighde, apparently in Armagh (*HDGP* vi, 125), and Colum Cille at Lissardowlan in Co. Longford. Beag mac Dé, who was noted for his prophetic powers, is also said to have foretold his birth. The homily of the vernacular Life also draws on the hymn in praise of Ciarán attributed to Colum Cille (cf. §33 below).

§1   *the people of Latharna in the region of Midhe.* The Latharna, who gave name to Larne in Co. Antrim, are otherwise unattested in the region of Midhe, which corresponds roughly to the present county of Westmeath and the north of Co. Offaly. The vernacular Life places the tribe more correctly in Ulster (*LisL* l. 3982), as does the commentary on Ciarán's feast in the Martyrology of Óengus, which locates the family among the Dál nAraidhe (*MartO* 202).

§1   *His father, called Beoaidh.* As Plummer has already pointed out (*Vitae*, I, xlviii; ii, 347), the forms of this name vary considerably, with no fewer than four to choose from in the saint's pedigree, viz. *Beo(dh)án*, *Baodán*, *Beoaidh*, and *Beonaidh* (*CGSH* §125.1). I follow Plummer in preferring *Beoaidh*. The vernacular Life, which also adopts this form, adds here the patronymic *Olcu* to Beoaidh's name (*LisL* l. 3982). The identification of Beoaidh as a *saor*, 'wright / carpenter', is one of many attempts to portray Ciarán in the image of Christ. Cf. Herbert, 'An infancy narrative'.

§1   *a wife named Dairearca.* The vernacular Life attaches the saint's mother through a father named Earcán to the Ciarraighe of Iorluachair (north-east Kerry) and, more specifically, to a tribe named Glasraighe (*LisL* l. 3989). The Annals of Clonmacnoise (*AClon.* 81) assign his mother to the descendants of Corc son of Fearghas son of Róch of the Ulster Clanna Rudhraighe.

§1   *Luiceann ... Donnán ... Odhrán ... Crónán the deacon.* Later in the Life (§23) Luiceann and Odhrán are placed in Íseal Ciaráin, near Clonmacnoise, where, according to the saint's vernacular Life, they were also buried. Donnán is said to have joined Ciarán in the graveyard at Clonmacnoise (*LisL* ll. 3998–9; Walsh, *Genealogiae*, 109).

§1   *Three daughters, named Luighbheag, Raichbhe and Pata.* The vernacular Life asserts that Ciarán's sisters were buried, together with their brother Crónán, in *Teach Mhic an tSaoir*, probably now Templemacateer in the Westmeath parish of Ardnurcher (*LisL* ll. 3999–4000; Walsh, *Placenames*, 255; Kehnel, *Clonmacnois*, 314; Walsh, *Genealogiae*, 109).

§1   *Ainmhire, king of Tara.* Ainmhire of the Ceinéal Conaill of Donegal is recorded as 'high-king' during the three-year period between 566 and 569 (*AU s.a.*). The vernacular Life wrongly names his father as Colga (*LisL* ll. 4001–2).

§1   *in the plain of Aoi.* This was the plain between Elphin and Rathcroghan in Co. Roscommon (*HGDP* i, 58–9).

§1   *Criomhthann the king.* No king of Connacht of that name is known. The vernacular Life (*LisL* l. 4004) identifies Criomhthann as a son of Lughaidh son of Dallán, king of Ireland. This Criomhthann is found among the Uí Mhaine, but he had no claim to kingship (Ó Muraíle, *Leabhar Mór*, 320.4.5.10). The name may have been extrapolated from the placename Ráith Chriomhthainn.

§1   *the druid of the aforesaid king.* Lughbhran is the name given to the druid in the vernacular Life (*LisL* l. 4007).

§1   *a holy deacon called Diarmuid in Irish, but later named Iustus (Just).* This deacon is known from Tíreachán's Life of Patrick, which, while adverting to the tradition that he baptized Ciarán, places him in Fiodharta, now Fuerty, Co. Roscommon (Bieler, *Patrician texts*, 128 (§7.2), 146 §28.1).

§2   *king Criomhthann's son Aonghas.* Aonghas is not known from any other source.

§2   *revive your horse.* The revival by saints of kings' horses is a common motif. Cf. Plummer, *Vitae*, i, 201 §2.

§2   *the place, which was both very good and large.* The vernacular Life names the place as *Tír na Gabhra*, 'Land of the Horse', but this is otherwise unattested (*LisL* l. 4027).

§3   *bring honey daily to their parents.* A very similar miracle is related in Patrick's Tripartite Life (Stokes, *Tripartite Life*, 14). For the value attached to bees and their honey, see Kelly, *Early Irish farming*, 108–10.

§3   *so that he might witness the miracle.* The vernacular Life (*LisL* ll. 4032–30) states that the honey was given as a reward to deacon Iustus.

§4   *This rock, which now has the cross of Christ on it.* The rock appears to be no longer there (Macalister, *The Latin and Irish Lives*, 113–14).

§4   The vernacular Life adds here three episodes of which one gives an account of how Ciarán rescued his book, called *Polaire Chiaráin*, from a tame fox which had begun to gnaw at it, and another describes how he first hindered and finally helped his mother to dye clothes (cf. Herbert, 'An infancy narrative').

§5   *collected its bones into his lap … the calf rose up in front of all.* A similar story is told in the late Irish Life of Colum Cille (O'Kelleher & Schoepperle, *Betha Colaim Chille*, §212); cf. Plummer, *Vitae*, i, cxliii; Macalister, *Latin and Irish Lives*, 117–18.

§6   *Lord, deliver not up to beasts the soul that trusts in thee.* The corresponding biblical passage is Psalms 73:19. The same passage is quoted in similar circumstances in Patrick's Tripartite Life (Stokes, *The tripartite Life*, 36)

§7   *from another territory.* The vernacular Life (*LisL* ll. 4090–1), while placing Ciarán in Ceinéal Fiachach – later mainly the Westmeath barony of Moycashel (*HDGP* iv, 123) – identifies the other territory as Uí Fhailghe – later equivalent to parts of east Offaly and west Kildare.

§9   *his uncle Beoán.* This man is otherwise unattested.

§9   *Clooncrim.* This place (Irish *Cluain Cruim*) is located in the Roscommon parish of Kiltullagh, formerly the greater part of the lordship of Uí Fhloinn, alias Síol Maolruain (*HDGP* v, 105). A lord of the family was killed there in 1464 (*AConn. s.a.*).

§11   *the home of king Furbhaidhe.* The vernacular Life has a corrupt form of the name, viz. Furban. The Life of Ciarán of Seirkieran (§§30–1) likewise alludes to the Clonmacnoise saint's period in servitude with Furbhaidhe, who kept him in chains, but the detail of the chapter is quite different.

§11   *Iarnán of the race of the Déise.* No such man is otherwise known but, if his name derives from *iarann*, 'iron', then the use of *gobhainn*, 'smiths', in the vernacular Life (*LisL* l. 4101) becomes more understandable.

§12   *a place called Cluain Innsythe.* This place has yet to be identified. A similarly named Cluain Infidhe, which was also on the river Shannon, has been tentatively identified as 'on or near Feenish' in south Clare (*HDGP* v, 127).

§12   *according to the western manner of Britain and Ireland.* This would appear to refer to the method of separating the grain of corn from the stem called *loiscreán* from *loscadh*, 'burning'. As Fergus Kelly points out (*Early Irish farming*, 240), this method was banned by statute in 1634.

§13   *food not given to guests in Christ's name was to be destroyed by men.* I know of no parallel to this maxim.

§15   *the school of Finnian.* This saint's school at Clonard was reputedly attended by numerous other saints, some of whom – namely 'two saints Ciarán, two saints

Bréanainn and Colum' – are here listed. A fuller list, including these saints and others, is recorded in the vernacular Life (*LisL* ll. 4121–5) and also in Heist, *Vitae*, 83 §5. Cf. Macalister, *Latin and Irish Lives*, 126.

§15 *that a cow be led by him to the school*. As against his mother's refusal of his request, a note on the saint's feast in the Martyrology of Óengus credits his father with allowing him to choose a cow from the herd (*MartO* 202).

§15 *Clonard on Leinster's border with Uí Néill*. The ridge on which Clonard stood was regarded as the boundary between Ireland's two Halves, north and south (Meyer, *Mitteilungen*, 293; *HDGP* v, 129).

§15 *a barrier … in the field … between the cow and its calf*. For other examples of this common motif, see Plummer, *Vitae*, I, xcvii note.

§15 *Odhar Chiaráin* (Ciarán's dun cow). The status of the cow's hide as a relic is elsewhere attested in a note to the saint's feastday in the Martyrology of Óengus (*MartO* 204; Kelly, *Early Irish farming*, 31–2). It also gave name to the earliest surviving vernacular manuscript, *Leabhar na hUidhre*, 'Book of the Dun Cow', written in Clonmacnoise, supposedly on the cow's hide, towards the end of the eleventh or early twelfth century (Joynt, *Tromdámh Guaire*, ll. 1282–4).

§16 *until a church for virgins be built for her*. A convent of Augustinian canonesses was founded at Clonard about the middle of the twelfth century under an abbess named Agnes, a daughter of the king of Tara, Murchadh mac Domhnaill Uí Mhaoil Sheachlainn (†1153). Her sister, Dearbhfhorghaill, became abbess of the Augustinian convent at Clonmacnoise (Gwynn & Hadcock, *Medieval Irish religious houses*, 314–15). The vernacular Life describes the girl as a daughter of the king of Cuala, an area covered roughly by south Dublin and north-east Wicklow (*LisL* l. 4128; *HDGP* vi, 146–7).

§16 *I never saw either her face or any other part of her*. The poem attributed to Cuimín of Connor states that Ciarán never looked at a woman from the time he was born (Stokes, 'Cuimmín's poem', 62; Macalister, *Latin and Irish Lives*, 126).

§17 *Ciarán read Matthew's gospel*. Ciarán's close association with this gospel-book is discussed above at p. 11.

§17 *Whatsoever you would that people should do unto you, do you likewise unto them*. This is 7:12 of Matthew's gospel. The vernacular Life (*LisL* ll. 4142–60), which uses the passage to justify Ciarán's loan of his book to Ninnidh Saobhroisc of Inismacsaint in Lough Erne, quotes the Latin text, before translating it. It also adds here the phrase: *non legam Marcum quousque compleueram Mattheum*, describing it as a famous saying brought to Alexander in Rome. Macalister (*Latin and Irish Lives*, 129) assumes that Pope Alexander II was intended. In the Martyrology of Óengus (*MartO* 202), Colum Cille is described as being present when Ciarán quoted the gospel verse. Cf. *DIS* 516.

§17 *Leath Matha.* There may be a play here on the name *Leath Mogha*, the southern Half of Ireland, over which Ciarán was given control. According to the Martyrology of Óengus (*MartO* 202), Colum Cille uttered the words *Leath Éireann*, which are rendered *leth cell Erind* in this saint's late vernacular Life (O'Kelleher & Schoepperle, *Betha Colaim Chille*, 128 §130).

§18 *ate bread on the third day.* For rules governing fasting, see Kelly, *A guide*, 182–3.

§18 At this point the vernacular Life adds several episodes. These include: an account of an amorous approach made to the saint by an erenagh's daughter; his resuscitation of a layman named Cluain; a prophecy made about him by Bréanainn of Birr, and his grant to Ninnidh of Inismacsaint of the dun cow he had brought to Clonard, on the understanding that the cow's hide would later be sent to Clonmacnoise (*LisL* ll. 4161–266).

§19 *Tuathal Maolgharbh, because he was rough.* One of two obits assigned to Tuathal places his death in the same year as that of Ciarán, viz. 549 (*AU* s.a. 544, 549). Two explanations of his cognomen, neither of which agrees with Ciarán's biographer, are provided by the text of *Cóir Anmann*, 'Fitness of names' (Arbuthnot, *Cóir Anmann*, i, 117, 184).

§20 *a frying-pan.* Latin *sartago*. This Latin term does not appear to have an Irish equivalent.

§21 *Ciarán went to the island of Aran.* A church and well on Inishmore were dedicated to the saint and, as Roderic O'Flaherty already noted in 1684, Ciarán was also patron of a church in the mainland Galway parish of Moyrus, opposite Aran (Hardiman, *A chorographical description*, 97; *OSL GY* iii, 115, 364–9). The vision seen by Ciarán is replicated in the Life compiled for Éanna, and is followed by a statement attributed to the Aran saint requesting of Ciarán that he take him and all his disciples under his protection. This may mean that Éanna's church on Aran was impropriate in some form to Clonmacnoise, which is where Éanna's Life was possibly compiled (Plummer, *Vitae*, ii, 72 §§26–7; *DIS* 281).

§22 *he gave him his hooded cloak.* The vernacular Life of Seanán locates this incident at a place called Uachtar Scéith, which has yet to be identified (*LisL* ll. 2388–9).

§22 *Seanán banished it to a certain distant lake.* The expulsion of the beast is discussed at length in Seanán's vernacular Life (*LisL* ll. 2194–236). The vernacular Life places the lake, which is called Dubhloch, on Sliabh Colláin, now Slievecallan in the Clare parish of Inagh (*HDGP* ii, 47 'Baile na Gréine').

§22 *Ciarán stayed for some days with Seanán, deliberating on the divine mysteries.* Deliberation of this kind is a common motif, especially in MT Lives. Cf. Plummer, *Vitae*, i, 56 §26.

§23 *Ciarán went to his brothers, Luiceann and Odhrán, who lived in a church called Íseal.* Íseal, alias Íseal Ciaráin, is mentioned several times in the annals, mostly in relation to the Clonmacnoise family of Mic Cuinn na mBocht, who appear to have kept a hospital there (*AClon.* s.a. 1069, 1087; *AFM* s.a. 1031, 1072, 1089, 1153; Swift, 'Sculptors and their customers', 116–17). The vernacular Life (*LisL* l. 4318) states that Cobhthach son of Breacán, who is otherwise unknown, gave the site to Ciarán.

§23 *Being older, Luiceann was the abbot of that place and Odhrán the prior.* See above at §1.

§23 *the open book was found bone-dry.* This is a stock motif; for other examples, see §26; cf. Macalister, *Latin and Irish Lives*, 142.

§24 *a chieftain and his attendants.* The vernacular Life (*LisL* ll. 4327–8) describes these as lay people and rabble.

§24 *both island and lake.* Only the island was moved, according to the vernacular Life (*LisL* ll. 4329–30).

§25 *a certain chieftain, namely Criomhthann's son.* The vernacular Life identifies the chieftain as Aonghas son of Criomhthann who, as was stated at §2 above, is not known from any other source.

§25 *taking on his shoulders satchels with books in them.* This is a most appropriate image for a saint whose church was noted for its learning.

§25 *satchels* (Latin *cethas*). Latin and Irish words for satchel have been discussed by Richard Sharpe (Sharpe, 'Latin and Irish words for "book-satchel"').

§25 *On reaching Lough Ree in east Connacht, the deer stopped opposite Hareisland.* The motif of a wild animal identifying the site of a saint's church is commonplace; it lent the site a sacred character (cf. Ó Riain, *Four Tipperary saints*, 50 §14, 73 §4). Hareisland (Irish Inis Ainghin) later hosted a priory of canons regular (Gwynn & Hadcock, *Medieval religious houses*, 177–8).

§25 *a certain priest by the name of Daniel.* The vernacular Life describes Daniel as a Briton (*LisL* l. 4345).

§25 *a very ornate gold ring.* The otherwise unattested Latin *antilum*, translated here as ring, is, as suggested by Macalister (*Latin and Irish Lives*, 145), probably a mistake for *annulum*. The vernacular Life reads *cuach*, 'goblet'.

§26   *Aonghas of the Laoighse*. Also known as Aona, this man died in 570, having
       held the abbacy for 26 years, according to the Clonmacnoise Annals of
       Tigernach. A different version of this story is given in a note to the Martyrology
       of Óengus (*MartO* 48–50), which locates the incident on Inis Clothrann, now
       Quaker Island, likewise the site of a priory of canons regular (Gwynn &
       Hadcock, *Medieval religious houses*, 178). See *DIS* 77.

§27   *The gospel-book was found to be bone-dry*. See note at §22. The vernacular Life
       (*LisL* l. 4359) suggests that this incident gave name to *Port an tSoiscéil*, 'Gospel
       Harbour', on Hareisland.

§28   *Donnán*. The vernacular Life (*LisL* ll. 4361–2) states that he was both the son
       of a brother of Seanán of Scattery, named Liath (Walsh, *Genealogiae*, 78), and
       a uterine brother of Seanán himself. However, Donnán is not among those
       listed as children of Seanán's mother, either in the tract on the mothers of the
       saints (*CGSH* §722.8) or in a poem on Fíonmhaith daughter of Baoth (*IrT* iv,
       93–4). Donnán was remembered on Hareisland on 7 January.

§28   *Hareisland with its effects*. According to the vernacular Life (*LisL* ll. 4366–7),
       the effects included the gospel-book rescued from the lake, a bell and its carrier,
       named Maol Odhráin.

§28   *Ard Manntáin*. Lying near the river Shannon, between Lough Ree and
       Clonmacnoise, this place has yet to be identified (*HDGP* i, 92).

§28   *[Ard] Tiobrad*. Written *Typrait* in the Latin Live, *Ard Tiprat* is the form favoured
       by the vernacular Life (*LisL* l. 4371). However, *Druim Tiobrad* is also attested
       in the story of the death of Diarmuid son of Cearbhall (O'Grady, *Silva Gadelica*,
       72).

§28   *Clonmacnoise*. The detailed description here provided of the church's location
       is in keeping with the approach of the MT redactor to his texts (Sharpe, *Medieval
       Irish saints' Lives*, 214).

§28   *he began to build a great monastery*. The vernacular Life enumerates the six
       present with the saint at the foundation as follows: Aonghas (alias Aona), Mac
       Nise, Caolcholum, 'Mulioc' (perhaps a mistake for Mobheóg, who is added to
       a separate listing), Lughna Maca Moghláimhe, and Colmán mac Nuin (*LisL*
       ll. 4375–6, p. 275n).

§28   *and both kings and chieftains of the Uí Néill and Connachta are buried there with
       holy Ciarán*. See pp. 8–9.

§28   *Ciarán then placed a post in the corner of the building*. The lower image on the
       shaft of the Cross of the Scriptures at Clonmacnoise, which shows two figures

holding a staff on the ground, has sometimes been taken to represent Ciarán and a king beginning to construct the church, but Peter Harbison (*The high crosses of Ireland*, i, 49, 202) puts forward a different explanation, involving the biblical figure Joseph. The vernacular Life states that Ciarán was accompanied by king Diarmuid son of Cearbhall when placing the post, before going on to claim that the post penetrated the eye of a disobedient man named Tréan from a place called Dún Cluana Íochtair (*LisL* ll. 4380–401).

§29 *the hooded cloak was then placed in the water of the river Shannon.* This episode is attached by the vernacular Life (*LisL* ll. 4310–16) to the story of Ciarán's visit to Seanán (§21).

§30 *Crithir of Clonmacnoise.* Plummer (*Vitae*, i, 212n) takes *crithir* to mean 'spark'; it could also mean 'tremble, quake' (*DIL* s.v.). The vernacular Life (*LisL* l. 4424) reads *Crichidh*.

§30 *Ciarán, a most holy aged bishop in the monastic town of Seir.* For the older Ciarán, patron of Seirkieran, whose Life also contains this episode, see pp. 47–8 (§32).

§30 *from Easter to Easter.* The Easter fire is an integral part of the liturgy surrounding this most important feast. As part of the vigil service the Paschal candle was lit and from it all other candles of the congregation were lit (*ODCC* 1226–7).

§30 *prophet who was killed by a lion.* This reflects the biblical passage 3 Reg. xiii.

§30 *The two Ciaráns then established friendship and fraternity … between those who followed after them.* As both churches later became locations of priories of canons regular, the fraternity underlying this part of the encounter between the two saints may echo this association. A prophecy similar to those recorded here regarding the future virtues of both monasteries is attributed to Ciarán of Clonmacnoise in the Life of Crónán of Roscrea (Ó Riain, *Four Tipperary saints*, 30 §5).

§31 *they became thirsty through the heat of the sun.* The same motif is used in the Life of Colmán Eala (§16).

§31 *Bringing drinking cups.* The form *cibaria* is used in the text, but I follow Macalister (*Latin and Irish Lives*, p. 38) in taking this to be a mistake for *ciboria*, 'drinking cups'.

§31 *Ciarán's last supper … because he lived afterwards for a few days only.* The claim is made in §31 that Ciarán lived for one year only in Clonmacnoise. It is not unusual for saints to be allowed a brief stay only, or none at all, in their principal churches. Another case in point is Colum who is allowed a glimpse only of Terryglass during his lifetime (Ó Riain, *Four Tipperary saints*, 14 §19, 89).

§31   *when Colum Cille and his community had come to Ireland on a visit from the island of Iona.* Adhamhnán (Anderson & Anderson, *Vita Columbae*, 14a–15b) gives a long account of Colum Cille's visit to Clonmacnoise at a time when Ailither (†599), who is described simply as Ciarán's successor, was abbot, but does not mention a 'great supper'.

§31   *Water that had been turned into wine.* As Macalister (*Latin and Irish Lives*, 154–5) points out, several saints are credited with changing water to wine, most notably perhaps, Colum Cille who, while a pupil of Finnian, performed this miracle and, by doing so as his first miracle, heightened the comparison with Christ's first miracle at the wedding feast of Cana (Anderson & Anderson, *Vita Columbae*, 324).

§31   *merchants came to him with wine from Gaul.* Plummer (*Vitae* I, c) cites some other examples of this form of trade, and Kelly (*Early Irish farming*, 319, 358–9) points to the regular trade there must have been in altar wine, as well as in wine for luxury consumption.

§32   *lived for one year only.* See previous chapter.

§32   *a stone pillow.* Ciarán's stone pillow, later known as *Adhart Chiaráin*, came to be regarded as a relic of the saint (above at p. 6).

§32   *This way is arduous.* The Latin Life reads *vita*, 'life', but, as the vernacular Life reads: *séad*, 'way', I follow Macalister (*Latin and Irish Lives*, p. 41) in reading Latin *via*, 'way'. The vernacular Life adds that both David son of Jesse and the apostle Paul dreaded the way. David's death is described in 3 Kings 2:1–9.

§32   *in the thirty-third year of his life.* As already stated (p. 3) his age at death is put variously at thirty-one, thirty-four and, Christ-like, at thirty-three. The likeness to Christ is a recurrent motif throughout the Life. Cf. Herbert, 'An infancy tale'. Having discussed the various annal entries concerning Ciarán, T.F. O'Rahilly (*Early Irish history and mythTology*, 235–6) concluded that the dates for the saint's life were either 512–44 or 517–49.

§32   *Caoimhghin of the province of Leinster.* The vernacular Life states that Ciarán marked the union by giving the other saint his bell, later named *Bóbán Caoimhghin* (*LisL* ll. 4470–1). The Annals of Clonmacnoise (*AClon.* 82) state that Ciarán ordained that his place of burial in 'the little Church of Clonnvicknos' should be shut with stones until Caoimhghin arrived. The two monasteries, Glendalough and Clonmacnoise, were closely linked. See Mac Shamhráin, 'The unity of Cóemgen and Ciarán'. Furthermore, both monasteries later hosted priories of canons regular (Gwynn & Hadcock, *Medieval religious houses*, 165, 177).

§32 *On the third night after Ciarán's death.* Ciarán's 'resurrection' on the third day after dying is once more a reminder of his likeness to Christ; cf. Macalister, *Latin and Irish Lives*, 160.

§32 *This is faithfully recounted at length in Caoimhghin's Life.* A comparison of the versions in the two Lives would suggest that Ciarán's biographer was drawing on the more extensive account in Caoimhghin's Life (See Plummer, *Vitae*, i, 248–9, §28).

§33 *many would be jealous of him.* According to both vernacular Life (*LisL* ll. 4472–76) and the note on his feast in the Martyrology of Óengus (*MartO* 204), the saints of Ireland came together 'and fasted for his death'.

§33 *Colum made a hymn for Ciarán.* A hymn in praise of Ciarán, taken to be that attributed to Colum Cille, has been preserved. It begins with the words *Alto et ineffabile apotolorum coeti* (Bernard & Atkinson, *Liber Hymnorum*, i, 157; ii, 218–20). Extracts from it are cited in the homily prefaced to Ciarán's vernacular Life (*LisL* ll. 3916–74; cf. Macalister, *Latin and Irish Lives*, 99, 165–6).

§33 *Coire Breacáin.* This dangerous marine whirlpool figures also in the Life of Colmán Eala (§13). Cf. Anderson & Anderson, *Vita Columbae*, 222.

§33 The vernacular Life ends with a long exordium, which begins with a reference to the jealousy of the saints of Ireland towards Ciarán, against whom they are alleged to have fasted to bring about a shortening of his life (*MartO* 204). There follows a list of some relics preserved in Clonmacnoise, and the exordium concludes with an extensive account of the saint's virtues (*LisL* ll. 4472–525).

THE LIFE OF CIARÁN OF SEIRKIERAN

§1 *the first-born of the saints of Ireland.* Ciarán is not only portrayed in this text as a pre-Patrician saint, he is also said to have died at the biblical age of three hundred (§39).

§1 *the western part of Leinster, the place called Ossory.* Historically part of Munster, Ossory was later alienated to Leinster (Byrne, *Irish kings and high-kings*, 181; Charles-Edwards, *Early Christian Ireland*, 569).

§1 *Luighne belonged to one of the more noble families of Ossory.* Ciarán's pedigree (*CGSH* §288) attaches him to the main line of descent of Ossory's kings, later represented by the Clann Mhic Ghiolla Phádraig (Fitzpatrick) family (O'Brien, *Corpus*, 117e39–g55).

§1   *a star fall into her mouth in a dream.* Similar motifs are used in relation to the births of Bréanainn of Clonfert, whose mother saw a bar of gold falling into her bosom (*CGSH* §716.2) and Fíonán, whose mother saw a golden fish entering her mouth (above, p. 81 (§1); Plummer, *Vitae*, ii, 87 §1). The Gotha Life of the saint places the event after Ciarán had already been conceived (Grosjean, 'Vita Sancti Ciarani', 225 §2).

§1   *Ciarán ... was born ... among the Corkalee, on Clear Island.* As the Life of St Finbarr also shows (Ó Riain, *Making of a Saint*, 84–7), there was thought to be a close relationship between the people of Ossory and the Corkalee (Corca Laoighdhe) of west Cork. A church was dedicated to Ciarán on Clear Island, and a church named Killyon (Ceall Liadhain) after his mother was located in the parish of Drumcullen, which adjoins Seirkieran (*HDGP* iv, 9).

§3   *thirty years ... without baptism.* This may echo the passage in Luke 3:23, which states that Jesus was about thirty when he was baptized by John.

§3   *he was ordained a bishop.* Ailbhe, another of the allegedly pre-Patrician saints, is also said to have been ordained bishop in Rome (Plummer, *Vitae*, i, 51 §14).

§3   *Pope Celestine.* See §7 below.

§3   *God kept the headship and total archiepiscopacy of Ireland for Patrick.* This claim is likewise made in the Life of Ailbhe (Plummer, *Vitae*, i, 54–5 §22). The meeting with Patrick is not in the *Salmanticensis* Life, but Patrick's Tripartite Life records a variant version of his encounter with Ciarán (Heist, *Vitae*, 347 §4; Mulchrone, *Bethu Phátraic*, 805–26).

§3   *Go to Ireland ahead of me.* This is designed to give Ciarán a pre-Patrician character. Patrick's role in directing Ciarán to the site of his future church is already attested in the Armagh saint's Tripartite Life (Mulchrone, *Bethu Phátraic*, ll. 821–6).

§3   *a well called Fuarán.* The name *(F)uarán*, 'little cold one', is sometimes used of wells, as is shown by 'Fooran Well' in the Offaly townland of Cannakill, near Croghan Hill (*AICO* §717; Hogan, *Onomasticon*, 660). The well in question is presumably that now known as St Kieran's well at Clonmore in the parish of Seirkieran. Significantly, this well lay on the west side of the Fuarawn river (*AICO* §725). Grosjean draws attention to the traditional etymology of the name *Saighir* as *saig*, 'seek', plus *uar*, 'cold' ('Vita Sancti Ciarani', 227–8n). The etymology is already present in a passage of Patrick's Tripartite Life (Mulchrone, *Bethu Phátraic*, l. 823).

§3   *on the confines of the northern and southern Irish.* Seir lay some miles south of the Slighe Mhór, which marked the boundary between northern and southern Irish (Ó Lochlainn, 'Roadways', 471)

§3   *bell … will be mute until you arrive at the … well.* This was a stock motif; for other examples, see Plummer, *Vitae*, I, clxxvii.

§4   *Bardán Ciaráin.* Literally meaning 'Ciarán's little bard', the name is described by Plummer (*Vitae*, I, clxxviii) as obscure. It is only attested in relation to Ciarán's bell (*DIL* s.v.). Grosjean ('Vita S. Ciarani', 229) gives a detailed account of the bell which, according to the author of the saint's Life, was still venerated in Ciarán's monastery. A gapped bell, called *Bearnán Ciaráin*, is mentioned in the annals (*ATig. s.a.* 1043) in relation to the community at Clonmacnoise.

§4   *bishop Gearmán, Patrick's teacher.* Patrick's seventh-century Life by Muirchú brings the saint to Germanus at Auxerre (Bieler, *Patrician texts*, 70 §1.6.1). There is no apparent connection between him and the monk named Gearmán in §29.

§4   *district called Éile.* This territory lay in the Offaly baronies of Clonlisk and Ballybritt; Seirkieran is in the barony of Ballybritt.

§5   *a most ferocious wild boar.* The presence of a wild animal at a site chosen for a church is a very common motif (Plummer, *Vitae*, I, clxxviii; Ó Riain, *Making of a saint*, 111).

§6   *the fox … stole his abbot's sandals.* Plummer (*Vitae*, I, clxi) described this episode as 'one of the most delightful things in hagiological literature'.

§7   *other three pre-Patrician saints.* Of the four so-called pre-Patrician saints, Ciarán is the only one who does not figure in all the other Lives; he is not mentioned in the Life of Ailbhe. For the most recent discussions of the pre-Patrician saints, see Sharpe, 'Quattuor sanctissimi episcopi'; Ó Riain-Raedel, 'German influence'.

§7   *Patrick … arrived in Ireland and … converted to Christ kings … and people.* As in the case of Ailbhe, Ciarán begins the conversion of the Irish, which is subsequently completed by Patrick (Plummer, *Vitae*, i, 54–5 §22; cf. §3 above).

§8   The Gotha Life places the Díoma episode later in its text (Grosjean, 'Vita Sancti Ciarani', 237 §9).

§8   *Ciarán's mother Liadhain.* See above at §1 and *DIS* 395–6.

§8   *a cell … in a nearby place.* Liadhain's church of Killyon (*Ceall Liadhain*) is in the parish of Drumcullen, which adjoins Seirkieran.

§8   *Broineach, the daughter of some Munster chieftain.* This may be the Broineach mentioned in the genealogies of the Uí Laoghaire of south-west Cork (*DIS* 129). Cf. Grosjean, 'Vita S. Ciarani', 237n.

§8   *Díoma, chieftain of … Uí Fhiachach.* The Uí Fhiachach, alias Ceinéal Fiachach, later 'Kenaleagh', controlled a kingdom in Westmeath corresponding roughly to the barony of Moycashel (*HDGP* iv, 123). Díoma is otherwise unattested.

§8 *the sound of a stork wakes me from sleep.* Latin *ciconia*, which normally means 'stork', becomes 'cuckoo' (Latin *cuculus* / Irish *cuach*) in the *Salmanticensis* version of the Life and in the second vernacular Life (Heist, *Vitae*, 348 §5; Plummer, *Bethada*, i, 116 §18). Miracles based on unseasonal occurrences are common in saints' Lives. For another example in this Life, see §16.

§8 *her belly decreased in size and the foetus disappeared.* Ruadhán of Lorrha is also credited with the termination of a pregnancy (Ó Riain, *Four Tipperary saints*, 77 §12).

§8 *Killyon.* See above (§1).

§9 *the chieftain came with bishop Aodh.* As already stated, Uí Fhiachach mainly comprised what is now the Westmeath barony of Moycashel. Aodh's church at Rahugh lay within this barony. For Aodh, see *DIS* 66–8.

§9 *Dúnchadh … was saved from the fire.* This son of Díoma is otherwise unattested.

§11 The Gotha Life places sections 10–11 later in its text (Grosjean, 'Vita Sancti Ciarani', 246–7 §§18–19).

§11 *twenty-seven white sheep.* White-fleeced sheep were highly prized (Kelly, *Early Irish farming*, 70).

§12 This section is omitted in the *Salmanticensis* Life. The Gotha Life places it later in its text (Grosjean, 'Vita Sancti Ciarani', 247 §20).

§12 *Fiontan brought his dead son Laoghaire.* This man is otherwise unknown.

§12 *Ráith Fheara.* Plummer (*Vitae*, ii, 338), following O'Donovan's note (*AFM s.a.* 816), identifies this as a probable reference to the townland and parish of Rahara in Co. Roscommon. Grosjean ('Vita S. Ciarani', 247n) tentatively proposes Rathsaran, earlier Ratharan / Rathfaran, in the Laois barony of Clandonagh, where there was a well dedicated to Ciarán.

§13 *Patrick … came to … Munster, where … Aonghas son of Nad Fraoich … believed.* Patrick's journey to Cashel is briefly recorded in the saint's earliest Lives but, unlike here, Ciarán neither figures in these texts, nor is there any reference to the theft of Patrick's horse (Bieler, *Four Patrician texts*, 163 §51.4; Mulchrone, *Bethu Phátraic*, ll. 2286–303). The Gotha Life inserts at this point a claim that Bréanainn of Birr was one of those who, influenced by Patrick, began to follow an eremitical life (Grosjean, 'Vita S. Ciarani', 231).

§13 *A certain man of the Uí Dhuach of Ossory, Mac Eirc by name.* The Uí Dhuach occupied lands mainly in the Kilkenny barony of Fassadinin (*ATig. Index* 192). The name of the man is corrupted to Maccersen in the Gotha Life (Grosjean, 'Vita Sancti Ciarani', 242 §13).

§13 *Carthach, Ciarán's disciple.* Variously described as nephew (or grandson) and son of Aonghas son of Nadh Fraoich, king of Cashel, Carthach is best remembered as patron of the Donegal church of Kilcar (*Ceall Charthaigh*). Cf. §24 and *DIS* 158–9.

§14 This section is omitted in the *Salmanticensis* Life. The Gotha Life places it later in its text (Grosjean, 'Vita Sancti Ciarani', 239 §10).

§14 *harpists who used sweetly sing songs about heroic deeds.* Playing the harp was the highest form of entertainment, but I know of no other reference to vocal accompaniment on the part of the harpist (Kelly, *A guide*, 64).

§14 *Múscraighe Tíre.* The people of this territory held lands in the Tipperary baronies of Upper and Lower Ormond, immediately south and west of the Offaly barony of Clonlisk, where Seirkieran was located.

§14 *many people fell asleep there.* Harpists were credited with the ability to bring on tears, joy, or sleep (Meyer, *Triads*, §122; Kelly, *A guide*, 64).

§14 *Loch na gCruitire.* The name does not appear to have survived.

§15 This section is omitted in the *Salmanticensis* Life and placed later in the Gotha Life (Grosjean, 'Vita Sancti Ciarani', 240 §11).

§15 *Múscraighe ... river Brosna.* For Múscraighe, see §14. The river in question is the Little Brosna, which rises in Slieve Bloom near Roscrea and flows into the river Shannon (*HDGP* ii, 202–3).

§15 *Carthach.* See §13. The first vernacular Life substitutes Mochuda for Carthach (Plummer, *Bethada*, i, 106–7 §§21, 25).

§15 *owner ... Eccanus.* This person, whom the vernacular Life calls Cáin, is otherwise unattested. The name Eccán, which occurs in *MartT* 34, is changed to Eogan in *MartG* 78. See Grosjean, 'Vita Sancti Ciarani', 240–1n.

§16 The Gotha Life places this later in its text (Grosjean, 'Vita Sancti Ciarani', 243 §14).

§16 *many mulberries.* For another miracle relating to unseasonal occurrences, see §8.

§16 *Conchradh, ruler of Ossory.* The vernacular Lives (Plummer, *Bethada*, i, 107 §27; 118 §33) name this man's father as *Duach / Danach*, which points, as in §13, to the Uí Dhuach of Ossory. Their pedigree (*CGH* 151a28–31) records a Conchradh son of Duach of Cliú in Ossory, an area now corresponding to the Carlow baronies of Idrone, which adjoin the Kilkenny barony of Fassadinin, formerly the lands of the Uí Dhuach (*HDGP* v, 73). Conchradh's daughter

Mughain gave name to Carn Mughaine in Airgeadros, a district lying mainly in the barony of Fassadinin (*HDGP* i, 46). For a recent discussion of this chieftain, see Connon, 'Territoriality and the cult of Saint Ciarán', 147–50.

§16 *Ciarán, whose parish was the whole of Ossory.* As patron of the diocese of Ossory, Ciarán had the whole of the territory as his *parochia*.

§16 *Aonghas was slain on the eighth of October.* It is unusual to have a date relating to a secular matter specified in this way. It may have some significance that a saint named Ciarán of Ráith Mhaighe, now possibly Rathmoy in the Tipperary parish of Glenkeen, was remembered on this day.

§16 *battle on Magh Fé in the province of the Leinstermen.* The battle of Magh Fé, also known as the battle of Ceann Losnadha, is dated to 490 (*AU s.a.*). The victor in the battle was Iollann (†527) son of Dúnlaing, king of north Leinster and the defeated were mainly the Uí Cheinsealaigh of south Leinster of whom Aonghas was an ally (cf. O'Brien, *Corpus*, 316c25–34).

§16 *the great monastic town of Kellistown (Ceall Osnadh).* Leighlin, which is located a few miles from Kellistown, is probably intended. Ceall Osnadh is a corruption of Ceann Losnadha (*HDGP* iv, 79–80).

§16 *Eithne Uathach ... daughter of Criomhthann son of Éanna Ceinsealach.* According to the genealogists (O'Brien, *Corpus*, 316c25), Eithne bore two sons to Aonghas, one of whom, Breasal, was a remote ancestor of Cormac son of Cuileannán who, coincidentally, was also slain in a battle in Leinster in 908, at Maigh Ailbhe, a plain in the Kildare barony of Kilkea and Moone.

§16 *Oilioll Molt, king of Ireland, in the ... battle of Oiche, in the kingdom of Midhe.* According to the annals for 482 / 483 (*AU s.a.*), Criomhthann, king of Leinster, was slain a year after Oilioll's death at the battle of Oiche, in which the victors were his cousins, Lughaidh son of Laoghaire and Muircheartach son of Earc (Byrne, *Irish kings and high-kings*, 85).

§17 The Gotha Life places this later in its text (Grosjean, 'Vita Sancti Ciarani', 246 §17).

§17 *archbishop Patrick.* The term archbishop would have been first appropriate in Ireland in the twelfth century.

§17 *God, who satisfied many thousands with a few loaves and fishes.* Christ's feeding of 5,000 on five loaves and two fishes, which is recorded in all four gospels, is probably intended (see Matthew 14:15–21).

§18 The Gotha Life places this later in its text (Grosjean, 'Vita Sancti Ciarani', 244–5 §15).

§18 *Oilioll, king of Cashel*. As no such king of Cashel is known, Plummer (*Vitae* ii, 339, 394) suggested that Oilioll Molt, king of Tara, might be intended. However, Aonghas of Cashel had a brother named Oilioll who became ancestor of the Eoghanacht Áine (O'Brien, *Corpus*, 148a40). Cf. §28.

§18 *Brosna*. The Little Brosna river formed a boundary of Munster (*HDGP* ii, 202–3). Cf. §15.

§19 The Gotha Life places this later in its text (Grosjean, 'Vita Sancti Ciarani', 245 §16).

§19 *A crowd of thieves*. The thieves are identified in the second vernacular Life (Plummer, *Bethada*, 118–19 §38) as Clanna Fiachrach, probably a corruption of the Uí Fhiachach mentioned in §8.

§19 *Lonán by name*. The second vernacular Life (Plummer, *Bethada*, i, 119 §38) takes him to be Lonán son of Nadh Fraoich, a brother of Aonghas, but no such person is otherwise recorded.

§19 *fiery ball ... from above*. Cf. §§24, 32.

§20 *a thief from Leinster by the name of Cairbre*. This man is otherwise unrecorded. Cf. Grosjean, 'Vita Sancti Ciarani', 231n.

§20 *Slieve Bloom*. The Little Brosna, which was regarded as a boundary of Munster, rose in Slieve Bloom (*HDGP* ii, 202).

§21 Sections 21–3 and 25–9 are omitted in the *Salmanticensis* Life. The Gotha Life places this and the two following sections later in its text (Grosjean, 'Vita Sancti Ciarani', 247–9 §§21–3).

§21 *sent oxen without a driver*. Miracles of this kind are commonplace. Cf. Plummer, *Vitae*, i, 59 §34).

§21 *his foster-mother Cóch (Coinche)*. This saint gave name to Kilcoe (Ceall Chóiche) in the Cork barony of West Carbery (*DIS* 178).

§21 *Rossmanagher*. Rossmanagher (*Ros Beannchair*) in the Clare parish of Feenagh was near enough to the 'western sea', and may be intended here. See *HDGP* iii, 89.

§22 *Habakuk to go from Judea to Caldea*. The biblical passage is Daniel 14:32–8.

§23 *A certain large stone, now called Cóch's stone*. Called *Carraig Chóiche* in Irish, this stone or rock stood presumably at or near Rossmanagher (*HDGP* iii, 89).

§23 *'God is wonderful in his saints'*. The reference here is to Psalm 67:36.

§24 The Gotha Life places sections 24–9 later in its text (Grosjean, 'Vita Sancti Ciarani', 250–7 §§26–37).

§24 *Ciarán's pupil Carthach*. See §13.

§24 *A ball of fire suddenly came down between them*. Cf. §§19, 32.

§25 *brothers named Odhrán and Meadhrán from ... Múscraighe Tíre*. Odhrán Maighistir, 'Master', of Latteragh in Co. Tipperary was the best known of the saints of this name. His church later became impropriate to the Augustinian canons of Toomyvara. His brother was known as Meadhrán Saighre, 'of Seirkieran' (*CGSH* §200; *DIS* 519). The advice he received from Ciarán is alluded to in the Life of Colum of Terryglass (Ó Riain, *Four Tipperary saints*, 17 §28).

§25 *Assaroe (Tulach Ruaidh) in the kingdom of Connacht*. Almost the same wording is used to describe the location of Tulach Ruaidh, at or near Assaroe, in the Life of Crónán of Roscrea (Ó Riain, *Four Tipperary saints*, 19 §2).

§25 *that place will be known by your name*. Leitreacha Odhráin is the usual designation of the site. See Hogan, *Onomasticon*, 487.

§25 *which are to be read in his Life*. This is the only mention of an otherwise unattested Life of Odhrán (Plummer, *Miscellanea*, 252).

§26 *a certain lady by the name of Eachall ... a district called Léim Eachaille*. Plummer (*Vitae*, ii, 326) identifies the place as probably the townland of Leap in the Offaly parish of Aghancon, which adjoins Seirkieran. The Gotha Life changes Eachall to Ethilda.

§27 *steward of the king of Munster by the name of Ceann Faoladh*. This man is otherwise unattested.

§27 *Ráith Mhaighe*. Plummer (Vitae ii, 338) suggests the townland of Rathmoy in the Tipperary parish of Glenkeen, which adjoins the barony of Eliogarty, formerly part of the territory of Éile.

§28 *Oilioll, king of Munster*. See note at §18.

§29 *a ... pilgrim named Gearmán*. In the Westmeath parish of Faughalstown, Diarmuid of Inchcleraun (Quaker's Island), who figures prominently in the Life of Ciarán of Clonmacnoise (§§1, 4), was sometimes called Gearmán (Walsh, *Placenames*, 53n). The first vernacular Life takes Gearmán of Auxerre to be intended (Plummer, *Bethada*, i, 109 §41). Cf. *DIS* 263.

§29 *Carthach, son of the king of Cashel*. See §§13, 24. The saint is usually described as the *nepos*, 'nephew / grandson', of Aonghas, king of Cashel.

§29 *as is read*. There is some confusion here; *fertur* is added above the line to give the sense of 'as is said'. The sentence refers back to §24.

§30 *king named Furbhaidhe*. The Life of Ciarán of Clonmacnoise (§11) also refers to his being imprisoned because of his charity by a king named Furbhaidhe but, there, his release was not brought about by the provision of red and white cows. The Gotha Life reads *Geranus* for *Ciaranus* (*Pyranus*) possibly because, as Grosjean ('Vita Sancti Ciarani', 233n) suggests, there was a Cornish saint named Gerent. Cf. Orme, *Saints of Cornwall*, 126–7.

§30 *cows, red of body but white of head*. While white cows with red ears are very often associated with saints, cows with red bodies and white heads do not appear to be mentioned elsewhere. Cf. Kelly, *Early Irish farming*, 31–4; Plummer, *Vitae*, I, cxlv.

§30 *The abbot Ciarán ... went to the ... elder bishop Ciarán*. The passage in the Life of Ciarán of Clonmacnoise (§30) that refers to Ciarán of Seirkieran also describes him as both elder and bishop.

§30 *The two saints Bréanainn*. The patrons of Clonfert, likewise the location of an Augustinian priory, and Birr are intended.

§30 *curds and pottage, fish, honey and oil; and wine a-plenty*. I follow Plummer (*Vitae*, ii, 382) in taking Latin *galmulum* to mean 'curds'. However, Grosjean ('Vita Sancti Ciarani', 234) takes it to mean a form of coagulated milk. All types of food and drink mentioned here are discussed by Fergus Kelly in his *Early Irish farming*.

§30 *certain former layman ... did not wish to eat*. The Life of Ruadhán (§21) provides another example of refusal to eat on the part of a former layman.

§30 *Mac Conghail*. This man is otherwise unattested. The Gotha Life corrupts the name to Maccanmael (Grosjean, 'Vita Sancti Ciarani', 234).

§30 *You will eat meat for sure during Lent*. For the consumption of meat during Lent, see Kelly, *Early Irish farming*, 344; cf. Plummer, *Vitae*, I, cxx.

§31 *the two Ciaráns and two Bréanainns, signed up to a friendship and fraternity*. Of the four saints, three were attached to churches that later became locations of Augustinian priories, namely Clonmacnoise, Seirkieran and Clonfert.

§31 *an abundance of riches ... an abundance of wisdom and religion*. For a similar prophecy relating to the future virtues of churches, see Ó Riain, *Four Tipperary saints*, 30 §5.

§31 *A place called Áth Salchair*. This ford was probably on the river Brosna (*HDGP* i, 152).

§31 *those animals were no longer visible*. The disappearance of miraculously supplied animals or other items is a common motif.

§32 Sections 32–4 are omitted in the *Salmanticensis* Life.

§32 *boy called Críchidh Cluana*. For this whole episode, compare the Life of Ciarán of Clonmacnoise (§30). There, however, the prayers of the younger Ciarán bring the boy back to life. The first vernacular Life (Plummer, *Bethada*, 110 §47) names the otherwise unknown boy as Trichemh.

§32 *the consecrated Easter fire*. See Plummer, *Vitae*, I, cxl–li.

§32 *a ball of fire fell from above*. See also §§19, 24.

§33 *one of the brethren, Baoithín by name*. This man is otherwise unknown. The second vernacular Life (§15) names him, corruptly, as *Bartanus* while the first substitutes a demon (Plummer, *Bethada*, 111 §50, 115 §15). *Baitanus* is the form of the name in the Gotha Life (Grosjean, 'Vita Sancti Ciarani', 236 §8).

§33 *Ruadhán ... of Lorrha*. See *DIS* 541–4.

§34 *Baoithín ... spilled a vessel full of milk*. For another example of spilled milk, see Ó Riain, *Four Tipperary saints*, 76 §10.

§35 The Gotha Life places this later in its text (Grosjean, 'Vita Sancti Ciarani', 257–8 §39).

§35 *the saint ... asked three requests of God*. The request for three petitions may be modelled on the three petitions attributed to St Patrick (Stokes, *Tripartite Life*, 331). For another example, see the Life of Colmán Eala (§50).

§35 *the people of Ossory, who accept him as patron*. Underlying this comment is Ciarán's position as patron of the diocese of Ossory.

§36 Sections 36–8 are omitted in the *Salmanticensis* Life.

§36 *went in old age to the most holy and wise Finnian*. As a pupil of Finnian, Ciarán also came to be regarded as one of Ireland's apostles (Heist *Vitae*, 83 §5; *CGSH* §712.6).

§37 The Gotha Life places sections 37–9 later in its text (Grosjean, 'Vita Sancti Ciarani', 258–62 §§40–1). Moreover, it brings him to Cornwall, where he then dies.

§38 *Now called Ciarán's well*. This may well refer to the holy well at Clonmore, adjoining Seirkieran (*AICO* §725). Cf. §4.

§39 *three hundred years in the flesh*. The saint's fabulous age at death is increased to three hundred and fifty in the *Salmanticensis* Life and four hundred in his second vernacular Life (Heist, *Vitae*, 353 §20; Plummer, *Bethada*, i, 122 §67). Cf. *MartD* 64.

§39 *on the fifth of March.* Ciarán's feast of 5 March, kept locally until modern times, was observed in many other churches throughout Ossory, including Kilkieran, Rathkieran, Tullaherin and Stonecarthy. The feast is shared by his pupil Carthach.

THE LIFE OF COLMÁN OF LYNALLY

§1 *the Uí Néill.* As already pointed out (p. 50), Colmán's descent elsewhere attaches him to a lowly rent-paying people of Dál nAraidhe named Maca Seille, and not to the Uí Néill.

§1 *the addition of Alo [Eala].* This anticipates the saint's choice of his place of resurrection at Lynally (Lann Eala) in a wood named Fiodh Eala (§14).

§1 *at a time of hostile devastation.* The M version of the Life, while placing the events in the kingdom of Midhe, attributes the devastation to the Leinstermen.

§1 *valley of Oichle.* The valley is in the Tyrone parish of Upper Bodoney. Cf. Reeves, *Acts of Archbishop Colton,* 55, 73.

§1 *as is usual with women when giving birth.* The M version omits the reference to those assisting.

§2 *a holy man named Cainneach Caomhán.* The M version omits the reference to Cainneach, as does the S version further on in the passage. The saint in question may be the associate of Patrick so named who became patron of the Derry parish of Kilrea (*DIS* 154–5). O'Hanlon (*Lives,* ix, 596) thought it might refer to Caomhán of Anatrim (*DIS* 155).

§3 *he set up a little monastery.* No indication is given by the S version as to where the little monastery was located. The M version locates his first church in Connor 'where Mac Nise lies', while asserting that Colmán, its 'second patron', lived there for a long time. It places this section after the saint had founded Lynally (Plummer, *Vitae,* i, 153 §3).

§3 *three of them were dead.* Cf. §18.

§3 *he raised the youth from the dead.* The MT version adds here: 'Lord Jesus Christ who raised Lazarus up after four days of decay' (Plummer, *Vitae,* i, 261 §6). The biblical passage is John 11:1–44.

§4 *Colmán … pierced a rock with his staff.* This is a stock motif, the biblical model being Moses in the desert, as described in Numbers 20:11 and Exodus 17:5.

§5   *I hear the voice of a son of life among these laymen.* See the Life of Ciarán of Clonmacnoise (§26) for another example of identification of saintliness by the sound of a voice.

§5   *Their lord Tuadán.* The MT version (§8) names this man as *Tuachnanus.* A branch of the Oirghialla took its name from a certain Tuadán (O'Brien, *Corpus*, 141b41).

§5   *Colmán Muilinn.* Colmán is said to have been a son of Brónach daughter of Míleac, Patrick's master. He was patron of the Antrim church of Derrykeighan (*DIS* 207).

§6   *when fear of famine affected the brethren.* For famine in early Ireland, see Kelly, *Early Irish farming*, 154–5. Cf. §§3, 15 of this Life.

§6   *butter and curds.* For the place of curds in the Irish diet, see Kelly, *Early Irish farming*, 327–8.

§8   *the river Main (Mion).* This river in the north-east of Ireland divided Ceinéal Eoghain from Dál nAraidhe (*MartO* 208). These may be the two peoples said here to be at war with one another.

§9   *the river Moyola (Bior).* The river Moyola, which forms the boundary of Fir Lí in the Derry barony of Loughinsholin, flows into Lough Neagh (*HDGP* ii, 147–8).

§10   Omitted in MT.

§10   *the river Blackwater (Dabhall).* This river, which forms the border between the present counties of Armagh and Tyrone, also flows into Lough Neagh.

§11   *the monastic town of Aodhán son of Aonghas.* Aodhán's 'great church' (*Ceall Mhór*) is now Kilmore in the barony and county of Monaghan. Cf. *DIS* 74.

§11   *at the hour of vespers on Saturday.* Vespers is the evening prayer, said at sunset, which, on Saturdays, might be felt to affect Sunday rest.

§11   *the day of the Lord is approaching.* Colmán is here enforcing the practice of resting from manual work on Sundays.

§12   Omitted in MT.

§12   *the church of holy Lasair.* The church is not identified but it seems to have lain near Armagh, in which case Donaghmoyne in Co. Monaghan may be intended (*DIS* 392). Plummer (*Vitae*, ii, 362) preferred Killesher in Co. Fermanagh.

§12   *when they found two serpents.* In the Life of Ailbhe poison placed in wine is turned into a serpent (Plummer, *Vitae*, i, 50 §12).

§12   *the coarb of the holy bishop Patrick.* The coarb is not named.

§13   Omitted in MT.

§13   *Coire Breacáin (Whirlpool of Breacán).* This was the name of a whirlpool between Rathlin Island and the coast of Antrim (*HDGP* vi, 22–3).

§13   *out of necessity that I came to this region.* This may be an oblique reference to the battle of Cúil Dreimhne, which was the traditional cause of Colum Cille's exile.

§13   *Doire Cal[g]ach.* It may be that Doire Calgach, a name used for Derry, was intended.

§13   *the cruet that he had left behind.* The miraculous return of items forgotten or left behind was a common motif.

§14   *the territory of the Uí Néill.* Although unspecified in the S version, the territory is taken by the MT redactor to have been Midhe, otherwise Westmeath, where the dominant group were the Clann Cholmáin.

§14   *Aodh Sláine, Aodh son of Ainmhire.* The names are phonetically spelt as *Ed* in the S version. Aodh (†598) son of Ainmhire belonged to the northern Uí Néill, whereas Aodh Sláine (†604), his successor as high-king, was of the southern Uí Néill.

§14   *Colum Cille, Cainneach.* See *DIS* 138–40; 211–14.

§14   *Fiodh Eala* (Wood of Eala). The name of both wood and church (*Lann Eala*) are supposed to derive either from the name of the local river or from the name of a woman (*MartO* 212). The river close to Lynally is now called the Clodiagh river.

§14   *Laisréan, Colum Cille's steward.* Laisréan's presence at the selection of the site would suggest that Durrow, which is located a few miles only from Lynally, had authority over it. Durrow was a seat of a priory of Augustinian canons from the 1140s onwards (Gwynn & Hadcock, *Medieval religious houses*, 154, 174–5).

§14   *praying, fasting.* The usual three-day fast is not specified here.

§15   *feast of the Epiphany.* Falling on 6 January, this feast was at a time when scarcity of food might well have occurred.

§16   *Baodán … belonged to the Ceinéal Cairbre.* This family gave name to the Kildare barony of Carbury of which the ruling family were the Uí Chiardha (*HDGP* iv, 107). Baodán, whom the MT version (Plummer, *Vitae*, i, 260 §5) calls Beagán (Becanus), is otherwise unattested.

§18 Omitted in MT.

§18 *material for making beer, but the yeast was dead.* See Kelly, *Early Irish farming*, 332–5.

§19 *a Briton who ... became angry with Colmán ... rose up to kill him.* Britons are sometimes treated in Irish saint's Lives as untrustworthy people; cf. Plummer, *Vitae*, i, 187 §45.

§20 *Pope Gregory of the city of Rome seated on the altar.* Pope Gregory died on 12.3.604. Paul Grosjean ('La mort de S. Grégoire') draws attention to a fourteenth-century spiritual treatise which uses this episode of Colmán's Life as an *exemplum*.

§20 *a pilgrim ... from the city of Rome.* Pilgrims more usually travelled in the opposite direction, from Ireland to Rome.

§20 *Colmán Dubhchuilinn.* The saint known as Colmán Dubhchuilinn was remembered on 24 November at various places, both in the west of Ireland and in Leinster (*MartG* 224).

§20 *school of the apostle John the Evangelist.* John, Colmán and the subject of learning are also brought together in the quatrain devoted to Colmán's feast in the Martyrology of Óengus (*MartO* 196; *MartO* 246). See also pp. 55–6.

§23 *one of his brethren, Collán by name.* This man, who is said by the MT version (Plummer, *Vitae*, i, 265 §18) to have been known as *Obediens* because of his humility, is otherwise unattested.

§24 Omitted in MT.

§24 *his brother, a son of Beoghain.* Colmán is not otherwise known to have had a brother.

§24 *painted the colour of hyacinth.* Antipathy on the part of a saint towards hyacinth is also attested in the Life of Ailbhe of Emly (Plummer, *Vitae*, i, 58 §30).

§25 Omitted in MT.

§25 *Mochuda came to the church of Molua of the Maca Oiche.* Mochuda's church at Rahan gave name to the parish adjoining Lynally in Co. Offaly, whereas Molua's church was at Kyle in Co. Laois. The Maca Oiche, alias Corca Oiche, occupied lands in the western part of the Limerick barony of Glenquin (*HDGP* vi, 74–5).

§25 *Mochuda placed two satchels full of books on his shoulders.* For another example of book-satchels being carried on shoulders, see p. 22 (§25).

§25 *Go ... to a nearby place called Rahan.* A similar account of how Mochuda became head of a community of monks at Rahan is given in his own Life (Plummer, *Vitae*, i, 177 §19). Colmán is mentioned several times in Mochuda's Life.

§26 *son ... of perdition ... son of life.* Cf above at §5.

§26 *Díoma Dubh.* The Connor saint of this name is intended (*DIS* 266).

§27 *a certain man by the name of Crónán.* There were many saints of this name but the one most likely to be intended here is Crónán, alias Mochua, of Timahoe in Co. Kildare, whose Life represents him as likewise ridding Colmán Eala of a demon (Plummer, *Vitae*, ii, 184 §2; *DIS* 469).

§28 Omitted in MT.

§28 *Mochuda came to Colmán.* As already seen in §25, Mochuda was patron of the neighbouring church of Rahan.

§28 *a shiny crow with a milky head.* Crows had a poor reputation in early Irish literature (Kelly, *Early Irish farming*, 191–2).

§29 *a church ... at the confluence of two rivers.* Churches were typically located in border areas, as is implied by the mention here of a confluence of rivers (Ó Riain, 'Boundary association').

§29 *to take his staff.* Staffs were frequently used to mark out the surrounds of a church.

§31 *a son whom you will call Ciarán.* This youth is otherwise unattested.

§32 *Colmán came to the king, Aodh Sláine.* According to §14, it was Aodh Sláine who granted Colmán the site of his church at Lynally.

§33 *the hymn of St Patrick.* The best-known hymn in praise of St Patrick is attributed to his disciple Seachnall, but Colmán is also credited with composing this hymn (Bernard & Atkinson, *The Irish Liber Hymnorum*, i, 3–13; cf. *DIS* 552–3). See p. 52.

§34 Omitted in MT.

§34 *The mother ordered one of her boys to kill the blind infant.* Infanticide was very common in the Middle Ages and by no means unknown in Ireland, as is shown by the penalties imposed by Adhamhnán (Meyer, *Cáin Adamnáin*, §§34–5).

§34 *his name was Ceallán Caoch.* Two saints of the name Ceallán are known. One of them was associated with the church of Fancroft in the Offaly parish of Seirkieran (*DIS* 162–3).

§35 Omitted in MT.

§36 *Cluain Caoin.* Despite the note in another version of the Life that places Cluain Caoin 'iuxta Dubliniam' (near Dublin), this church may be the now obsolete 'Clonkeene' in the parish of Rahan, which adjoins Lynally (*HDGP* v, 95–7).

§36 *Dún Salach.* This lay in or near the territory known as 'na Comainn', which stretched from the eastern boundary of Laois to Slieve Bloom in Co. Offaly (*HDGP* vi, 32; cf. Hogan, *Onomasticon*, 389).

§37 Omitted in MT.

§37 *bread was being baked in the oven.* For an account of bread and baking in Ireland, see Kelly, *Early Irish farming*, 322, 330.

§37 *holding ... in his hand ... the fire.* Miraculous indifference to fire is commonplace in saints' Lives. See also the Life of Fíonán §35.

§38 Omitted in MT.

§38 *Molua of the Maca Oiche came to Colmán Eala.* Cf. §25.

§39 Omitted in MT.

§39 *Brannabh, king of Leinster ... a friend of Aidan of Ferns.* Brannabh son of Eacha, an Uí Cheinsealaigh king of Leinster, is said to have been killed in 605 by his own people in treachery (*AU s.a.*). Aidan, alias Maodhóg, of Ferns does not appear to have had any other association with the Offaly area or, more specifically, with Colmán, but Molua figures in Maodhóg's Life, as does the story of Brannabh's slaying (Plummer, *Vitae*, ii, 148–50 §§24, 26).

§39 *Colmán came to Clonfertmulloe.* Despite his close association with Killaloe, Molua's principal church was Clonfertmulloe, alias Kyle (*DIS* 490–3).

§40 Omitted in MT.

§41 *Colmán had come to Clonard.* This church, located on Leinster's boundary with Midhe (Westmeath/Offaly), had Finnian, a much more important saint than Colmán, as its patron (*DIS* 319–21).

§42 Omitted in MT.

§42 *the page was no sooner written than it dried.* Writing on vellum normally dries slowly.

§42 *a prophet ... like Colum Cille.* This saint was noted for his prophetic powers (*DIS* 214).

§43 *Colmán had come to Clonmacnoise.* As at Clonard, Clonmacnoise became the location of an Augustinian priory in the course of the twelfth century.

§43 *as if it were a feastday.* This may imply that sermons were otherwise normally confined to feastdays.

§44 *Comna.* The S Life reads *Canina*, whereas the MT version has Comna. The correct form of this name is more likely to be *Cuman*, gen. *Cuimne / Comna*. The genitive form adopted by the hagiographer may have been borrowed from a church name like *Ceall Chomna* or *Teach Comna*, now Kilcumny and Stacumny.

§44 *Bréanainn son of Cairbre.* The only person of this name recorded by the genealogists belonged to the Uí Mhaine (O'Brien, *Corpus*, 145f24).

§45 *water ... changed into a good beer.* Beer is already shown to have been prized at §18.

§46 *a journey in Connacht.* Why Colmán was brought to Connacht is unclear, unless it had to do with the rise to power of that province during the twelfth century. Cf. §47

§46 *it being customary in those days to kill females.* Heavy penalties were introduced for the killing of women in the *cáin*, 'law', attributed to Adhamhnán (Meyer, *Cáin Adamnáin*, §§34–5). Cf. Kelly, *Guide to early Irish law*, 79.

§47 *Blessed are the undefiled in the way.* The biblical passage is Psalm 119:1–2.

§47 *who had neither eyes nor nostrils.* 'Board-faced' people are sometimes mentioned in saints' Lives, the best-known example being Mobhí of Glasnevin (Plummer, *Vitae*, I, cxi).

§49 *he travelled to Clonard.* Why Colmán chose to consult Finnian on his wish to die is not made clear. In keeping with the representation of Finnian as already dead, his obit of 549 is separated by sixty years from that of Colmán in 609.

§50 *Mochuda of Rahan and other holy men.* This is the last of several mentions of Mochuda in the Life. Cf. §§25, 28.

§50 *these are the requests which the Lord has granted to me.* The requests number three, as do those allowed to Ciarán of Seirkieran (p. 48 §35).

§50 *he set free his soul and was buried.* This is an unusually brief description of the saint's death.

§51 *After Colmán's death.* Accounts of posthumous miracles are not common in Irish saints' Lives.

§51 *Colmán's staff.* The efficacy of the saint's staff is again illustrated in §§4, 29.

§52 *that his bones be elevated from his grave ... lest they be stolen.* The elevation of a saint's remains and their enshrinement was a common occurence. The whereabouts of Colmán's shrine are now unknown.

THE LIFE OF FÍONÁN OF KINNITTY

§1   *Fíonán ... Corca Dhuibhne ... Mac Airdhe ... Beagnaid.* The early vernacular Life (Br; Stowe) adds the saint's pedigree as follows: *Finan mac Cairrde mic Corcrain mic Nuidhin mic Irchuind mic Corbmaic mic Cuirc Duibhne mic Coirpri Músc mic Conaire mic Mogha Lama.*

§1   *This is how he was conceived.* Much the same story is told in verse in the Commentary on Fíonán's feast in the Martyrology of Óengus (*MartO* 112). There she is said to have been bathing in Loch Léin (Killarney Lower Lake), whereas the vernacular Life asserts that the fish came to her in a dream.

§1   *a wise and religious man.* The late vernacular Life (Macalister, 'Life of Saint Finan', 550 §1) identifies this man as Críod(h)án, possibly the saint of that name associated with Kilcredane, a parish in the Kerry barony of Magunihy.

§2   *her spittle cured every illness.* For the curative power of spittle imbued with holiness, see also the Life of Ruadhán (Ó Riain, *Four Tipperary saints*, 77 §12).

§3   Omitted in MT.

§3   *Calves ... ran off to the cows ... Fíonán dragged his staff ... along the ground.* A similar story is told in Ailbhe's Life (Plummer, *Vitae*, i, 49 §8). Separation of calves from cows was a common practice (Kelly, *Early Irish farming*, 39–40, 170). The author of the late vernacular Life cites as a parallel God's separation of the waters to save the people of Israel from being drowned (Macalister, 'Life of Saint Finan', 550 §1; cf. Exodus 14:21).

§4   *Bréanainn of the Maca Alta.* Like Fíonán, Bréanainn was of Kerry origin, and his main local church there was at Ardfert. His principal church was, however, at Clonfert, across the river Shannon from Co. Offaly (*DIS* 115–17). Maca Alta is a variant form of the tribal name Altraighe, a group that held lands in the Kerry baronies of Iraghticonnor and Clanmaurice (Ó Corráin, 'Studies', 31).

§4   *for seven years over the oven.* As Heist (*Vitae*, 153n) explains, there is some confusion in the wording of the text at this point, possibly due to haplology. As it stands, the sentence makes little sense.

§6   *he put his hand into ... the fire.* Indifference to fire is common in saints' Lives. Cf. the Life of Colmán Eala §37.

§7   *Fíonán ... come out and give him the Eucharist.* It is not stated how old Fíonán was at this point but, by the next chapter, he was already old enough to found a monastery. In any case, under Canon Law an acolyte was permitted to distribute Holy Communion.

§8   *the fire you see is the grace of holy Fíonán.* There is another example of this common motif in Mochaomhóg's Life (Ó Riain, *Four Tipperary saints*, 47 §7; cf. Ó hAodha, *Betha Brigte*, 1 §1; *LisL* ll. 1911–26).

§9   *I am junior to you.* For the possible meaning of this comment, see p. 79.

§9   *the mountain of Sinór, where you will find a herd of wild pigs.* The spelling of the name varies between *Sinór* and *Smór*. The MT and early vernacular versions of the Life add a note identifying the mountain as Slieve Bloom, the name given to the mountain in the R version and in the late vernacular Life (Plummer, *Vitae,* ii, 88 §8; Br; Stowe; Macalister, 'Life of Saint Finan', 552 §2). The presence of wild animals at a site chosen for a church is a common motif (cf. pp. 53, 82).

§9   *Kinnitty.* The name, more properly *Ceann Eitigh*, is spelt corruptly in S as *Kenn hIttich* (*HDGP* iv, 76). The MT version adds several sentences, which read in translation: 'The place is in the middle of Ireland, on Munster's border with the kingdom of Midhe, but located within the territory of Munster, and there he built a famous monastery called Kinnitty. Once the fame of his holiness was heard, a large community of monks developed under him, and he went on to found monasteries and churches in his own kingdom, that is Corca Dhuibhne, where he performed great wonders and miracles in Christ's name'. The early vernacular version adds much the same passage (Br; Stowe).

§10   *no layman dares to eat that place's butter.* Butter was a luxury food, which, according to the law tract *Críth Gablach*, a low-ranking person was not entitled to receive when visiting (Kelly, *Early Irish farming*, 326).

§11   *a raft.* The MT and vernacular versions prefer *navis / long / coite,* 'boat, canoe', to *ratis*, 'raft', in the S version.

§11   *the island on which Fíonán was.* The location on Loch Léin, now Killarney Lower Lake, indicates that the island in question was Inisfallen. Later the seat of a priory of canons regular, Inisfallen was also a centre of Fíonán's cult (Gwynn & Hadcock, *Medieval religious houses*, 180).

§11   *the king of Loch Léin, Feidhlimidh by name.* The king in question is very probably Feidhlimidh son of Aonghas son of Nadh Fraoich, whose descendants Fáilbhe Flann and Carthach – eponymous ancestor of the powerful Munster family of Mic Carthaigh (Pender, 'The O Clery Book of Genealogies', §2020) – are mentioned later in the Life (§§26–7). R and the late vernacular version omit the name of the king.

§11   *Loch Luighdheach.* This is now Lough Currane, near Waterville in Iveragh, likewise a centre of devotion to Fíonán. Unlike R, which places the event at Loch Léin, the late vernacular Life (Macalister, 'Life of Saint Finan', 554 §3) maintains that the canoe was built at Lough Currane. Neither the MT version nor the early vernacular version identify the place to which the boat was brought, but an island on Lough Currane – Oileán an Teampaill – contained a church dedicated to Fíonán (Seabhac, *Uí Ráthach*, 36).

§12 This is neither in MT nor in the early vernacular Life, but S shares it with both the late vernacular Life and the R version (Macalister, 'Life of Saint Finan', 554 §4).

§12 *Lonán son of Finneach.* Lonán belonged to the Éile, whose territory mainly comprised the baronies of Ballybritt and Clonlisk in Co. Offaly (O'Brien, *Corpus*, 154a28); Kinnitty is in the barony of Ballybritt. Lonán later figures in the pedigree of the Uí Chearbhaill (O'Carrolls) (Pender, 'The O Clery book of genealogies', §2045). R and the late vernacular version omit the patronymic.

§13 *in the lands of the Munstermen.* Both MT and the early vernacular Life add here: 'namely Corca Dhuibhne' (Plummer, *Vitae*, ii, 89 §11; Br; Stowe). This brings Fíonán back to south-west Munster. R and the late vernacular version omit the reference to Munster.

§13 *A holy man who loved God.* The late vernacular version omits this description.

§13 *Mac Gairbhe.* The name of this otherwise unattested man is common to all versions of the Life, except R and the late vernacular Life, which omit the name.

§13 *a beautiful calf came from on high.* The MT and early vernacular versions add that the mother rejoiced and gave a bellow to show its affection for the calf.

§14 *Fíonán's horse died.* MT and the early vernacular Life lead off with the statement that Fíonán had two horses on that road, one of which died. The late vernacular Life states that the leg of one of Fíonán's carriage horses broke (Macalister, 'Life of Saint Finan', 554 §4).

§14 *hyacinth-coloured horse with a white head.* Antipathy towards hyacinth colour is instanced in the Lives of Ailbhe (Plummer, *Vitae*, i, 58 §30) and Colmán Eala (§24). White was apparently the most prestigious colour of horses (Kelly, *Early Irish farming*, 91–2) but this one has an Otherworld character. The early vernacular Life substitutes the colour red for hyacinth (Br; Stowe).

§15 This is in neither MT nor the early vernacular Life, but it is in both R and the late vernacular Life (Macalister, 'Life of Saint Finan', 555–6 §5).

§15 *tree ... across the road.* For a similar miracle, see the Life of Crónán of Roscrea (Ó Riain, *Four Tipperary saints*, 35 §22).

§16 This is omitted in R and the late vernacular Life.

§16 *at the boundary of Corca Dhuibhne, at Ráith Maca Lapa.* Despite Ailbhe Mac Shamhráin's tentative identification of the place with Ralappane in the north Kerry parish of Kilnaughtin (Mac Shamhráin, 'Fínán Camm'), Ráith Maca Lapa, which is also mentioned at §20, was presumably located near the coast towards the west of Iveragh. The early vernacular Life substitutes *Ceapach na gCopóg*, which it further identifies as *Ceall Imleach,* now Killemlagh, of which Fíonán was patron; the editor of the Stowe version substitutes *Gort na gCopóg* and identifies it as 'na Dalks'. The Maca Lapa are otherwise unattested.

§17 This is neither in MT nor in the early vernacular Life, but it is in R and the late vernacular Life (Macalister, 'Life of Saint Finan', 556 §5).

§19 This is in no other version.

§19 *Fíonán was living on some island.* Church Island on Lough Currane may be intended.

§20 *When Fíonán was at Ráith Maca Lapa.* R and the late vernacular version omit the name of the place. Cf. §16.

§20 *turn the sod near him.* The late vernacular version substitutes a blow on the ground of Fíonán's staff.

§21 *Corca Dhuibhne were in distress for fear of ... the Fidhgheinte.* See p. 79.

§21 *for cursing.* The Latin text reads *ad catacominationem*, which Plummer explains (*Vitae,* ii, 381) as a compound of *cominatio* 'curse'. R and the late vernacular Life speak of blessed water (Macalister, 'Life of Saint Finan', 556 §6).

§21 *Neachtan son of Ceannfhada.* Sometimes styled Neachtan Ceannfhada or, in an earlier form, Neachtan 'cennocht' (O'Brien, *Corpus,* 149a26; 152a6), this man is found in the main pedigree of the Uí Fhidhgheinte. Neachtan Ceannfhada also figures in the vernacular Life of Seanán of Scattery Island, which presents him much more positively (*LisL* ll. 2350–69).

§21 *they had previously seen ... on fire.* Miracles involving the false appearance of fire are very common.

§21 *Diarmuid, king of the Uí Néill.* Diarmuid (†565) son of Cearbhall is probably intended, as both R and the author of the late vernacular Life also assumed (Macalister, 'Life of Saint Finan', 558 §6).

§22 This is neither in MT nor in the early vernacular Life, but it is in R and the late vernacular Life (Macalister, 'Life of Saint Finan', 558 §8).

§22 *the man walked in three hours.* This is a common motif. For another example of exceptional speed, see Ó Riain, *Four Tipperary saints,* 57 §25.

§23 *Fíonán's brother came to Kinnitty.* A brother of the saint is otherwise unattested. The early vernacular Life states that the saint's brother came from Kinnitty to Fíonán in Corca Dhuibhne, where he also woke from his sleep, while the late vernacular Life describes the saint's brother as a *thighearna duthaigh*, 'lord of his country' (Fáinne Fionn, 'Beatha Fionáin', 660; Macalister, 'Life of Saint Finan', 558 §9).

§23 *the equivalent of seven female servants.* Seven female slaves or its equivalent (Irish *cumhala*, Latin *ancillae*) was the honour-price of a king (cf. Kelly, *A guide*, 112–13). The late vernacular Life changes seven to eight, whereas the early vernacular Life specifies a *tuarastal*, 'stipend' (Macalister, 'Life of Saint Finan', 558 §9; Br; Stowe).

§24 *not a drop touched his harvesters from morning to evening.* This is a very common motif, as can be seen below at §31, and the Life of Ciarán of Clonmacnoise (§22).

§25 This is neither in MT nor in the early vernacular Life, but it is in both R and the late vernacular Life (Macalister, 'Life of Saint Finan', 560 §10).

§25 *a captive being led off to be killed.* As can be seen from §29 and many other examples, intercession by a saint on behalf of a captive is a common motif.

§26 *Treadhua of the Kings.* This was one of a large number of seats of the kings of Cashel. John O'Donovan (*Leabhar na gCeart*, 89, 93) explained the name as 'triple-fossed fort of the kings' and identified it, with no other support, with a fort at Kilfinnane in Co. Limerick. In the list, the name lies between Druim Fínghin, now a ridge extending from Fermoy to the Waterford coast, and Ráith Eirc, which is unidentified. The form *Tredhua* occurs also in names associated with Tara and Teltown (see Hogan, *Onomasticon*, 645). MT and the early vernacular versions substitute Cashel, while the late vernacular Life, but not R, describes Fáilbhe as king of Corca Dhuibhne (Macalister, 'Life of Saint Finan', 560 §11).

§26 *Fáilbhe Flann.* As with Feidhlimidh (§11) and Carthach (§27), this name also occurs in the genealogy of the Mic Carthaigh (Pender, 'The O Clery book of genealogies', §2020). See p. 79.

§27 *Carthach.* Carthach was the name of the eponymous ancestor of the Mic Carthaigh. See also the notes on Feidhlimidh (§11) and Fáilbhe Flann (§26).

§27 *a year and a half.* The MT version reads *anno uno*, 'one year'.

§27 *Fíonán made a sandal for him.* A single sandal represented a symbol of sovereignty, as is shown by the phrase *fear aonasa*, 'man of the single sandal', i.e. chieftain, man of high rank (Mac Airt, *Leabhar Branach*, 29 (l. 750), 347).

Unlike R, which reads *calciamentum*, 'shoe', the late vernacular version substituted *triubhas*, 'trousers', for sandal (Macalister, 'Life of Saint Finan', 560 §12).

§29 *upon which he was … struck dumb.* This is a stock motif; cf. §25.

§30 *the region of Ciarraighe Luachra* (MS *Diurgi*). Mention of Sliabh Luachra suggests that Ciarraighe Luachra, a region which comprised the greater part of north Kerry, is intended (*HDGP* iv, 145–7). R and the late vernacular version omit the name of the district.

§30 *Sliabh Luachra.* This was the mountainous area in the Kerry baronies of Magunihy and Trughanacmy and the adjoining Cork barony of Duhallow (*ATig. Index* 163). The name is omitted in all other versions.

§31 This is neither in MT nor in the early vernacular Life, but it is in both R and the late vernacular Life (Macalister, 'Life of Saint Finan', 562 §14).

§31 *games in Raithleann.* As John Lyons was the first to show ('Notes and queries: Raithlenn'), the placename refers to a cluster of fortifications in the townland of Garranes, parish of Templemartin, Co. Cork. The seat of kingship of the Uí Eachach of Munster, a branch of the Eoghanacht, which at times controlled the kingship of all Munster, was located here. R and the late vernacular version omit the name of the place.

§31 *great fall of rain.* See note to §24.

§32 *Mocheallóg.* There were several Kerry dedications to Mocheallóg, one at Kilmakilloge in the parish of Tousist in Iveragh – the site probably intended here – and three on the Dingle peninsula (*DIS* 461–2).

§32 *a white, red-eared calf.* Osborn Bergin ('White red-eared cows') drew attention to a still surviving old English breed of cattle having these typical colours of miraculously produced animals. R and the late vernacular version omit the reference to the colour of the ears. Cf. Kelly, *Early Irish farming*, 33–4.

§33 Neither R nor the late vernacular Life have this section.

§33 *the head of an onion.* The curative quality of onions does not appear to be attested elsewhere in the literature (Kelly, *Early Irish farming*, 251–3).

§35 *In a place near Lough Currane.* The place in question, is named *Inis Ussailli* in the MT version and *Inis Uasal*, alias *Inis na bhFear Naomh*, in the early vernacular Life (Plummer, *Vitae*, ii, 95 §26; Br; Stowe). Both R and the late vernacular version omit the placename (Macalister, 'Life of Saint Finan', 560 §15). It probably refers to Church Island on Lough Currane, and is cited as an alternative name for the parish of Dromod in a fifteenth-century annate relating to the diocese of Ardfert (*Archivium Hibernicum* 21, 7).

§35   *the smith's pincers.* MT and the early vernacular Life speak of a broken vessel.

§35   *took hold of the hot metal.* Miraculous indifference to heat is again claimed in the Life of Colmán Eala §37.

§36   *three fish from the waterless field.* I know of no other example of fish being miraculously caught on dry land.

§37   *the day of his death.* The MT version specifies the date of the saint's death as 'the seventh of the ides of April', i.e., 7 April. The early vernacular Life, as in Br and Stowe, omits the final chapter, with both scribes commenting that they could find no more of the Life.

Bibliography

Anderson, A.O. & M.O. Anderson (eds), *Vita Sancti Columbae: Adomnán's Life of Columba* (revised ed.; Oxford, 1991).

Arbuthnot, S. (ed.), *Cóir Anmann: a late middle Irish treatise on personal names*, 2 vols (Irish Texts Society 59, 60; London, 2005, 2007).

Atkinson, R. (ed.), *The Book of Ballymote*, Photo-lithogr. facsimile, with Introduction by R. Atkinson (Dublin, 1887).

Bergin, O.J., 'White red-eared cows', *Ériu*, 14 (1946), 170.

Bernard, J.H. & R. Atkinson, *The Irish Liber Hymnorum*, 2 vols (Henry Bradshaw Society 13–14; London, 1898).

Best, R.I., 'The Leabhar Oiris', *Ériu*, 1 (1904), 74–112.

Best, R.I., 'Graves of the kings at Clonmacnois', *Ériu*, 2 (1905), 163–71.

Best, R.I. & O. Bergin (eds), *Lebor na hUidre: Book of the Dun Cow* (Dublin, 1929).

Bhreatnach, E., 'Learning and literature in early medieval Clonmacnoise' in H.A. King (ed.), *Clonmacnoise Studies*, 2 (2003), 97–104.

Bieler, L., *The Patrician texts in the Book of Armagh* (Scriptores Latini Hiberniae 10; Dublin, 1979).

Bradley, J., 'The monastic town of Clonmacnoise' in H.A. King (ed.), *Clonmacnoise Studies*, 1 (1994), 42–55.

Bradley, J., 'Pulp facts and core fictions: translating a cathedral from Aghaboe to Kilkenny' in E. Purcell, P. MacCotter, J. Nyhan and J. Sheehan (eds), *Clerics, kings and vikings: essays on medieval Ireland in honour of Donnchadh Ó Corráin* (Dublin, 2015), 169–84.

Byrne, F.J., *Irish kings and high-kings* (London, 1973).

Carney, J., *The problem of St Patrick* (Dublin, 1973).

Carney, J., '*A maccucáin, sruith in tíag*', *Celtica*, 15 (1983), 25–41.

Carrigan, W., *The history and antiquities of the diocese of Ossory*, 4 vols (Dublin, 1905; repr. Kilkenny, 1981).

Charles-Edwards, T.M., '*Érlam*: the patron-saint of an Irish church' in A. Thacker & R. Sharpe (eds), *Local saints and local churches in the early medieval West* (Oxford, 2002), 267–90.

Charles-Edwards, T.M., *Early Christian Ireland* (Cambridge, 2000).

Colgan, J., *Acta sanctorum veteris et majoris Scotiae seu Hiberniae ... sanctorum insulae*, i (Louvain 1645; repr. Dublin, 1947).

Connon, A., 'Territoriality and the cult of Saint Ciarán of Saigir' in T. Ó Carragáin & S. Turner (eds), *Making Christian landscapes in Atlantic Europe: conversion and consolidation in the early Middle Ages* (Cork, 2016), 109–58.

De Brún, P., 'Kerry diocese in 1890: Bishop Coffey's survey', *Journal of the Kerry Archaeological and Historical Society*, 22 (1989), 99–180.

Doble, G.H., *Saint Perran, Saint Keverne, & Saint Kerrian* (Cornish Saints Series 29; Exeter, 1931).

Doble, G.H., 'The history of the relics of Saint Piran of Perranzabuloe', *Old Cornwall*, 3 (1942), 501–6.

Doherty, C., 'The cult of St Patrick' in J.M. Picard (ed.), *Ireland and Northern France*, (Dublin, 1991), 53–94.

Dubois, J. (ed.), *Le martyrologe d'Usuard: texte et commentaire* (Subsidia Hagiographica 40; Brussels, 1965).

Fáinne Fionn, 'Beatha Fionáin', *Irish Rosary* 15 (1911), 603–4; 659–60; 771–2.

FitzPatrick, E. & C. O'Brien, *The medieval churches of County Offaly* (Government of Ireland; Dublin, 1998).

Forbes, A.P. (ed.), *Kalendars of the Scottish saints* (Edinburgh, 1872).

Grosjean, P., 'Vita Sancti Ciarani Episcopi de Saigir ex Codice Hagiographico Gothano', *Analecta Bollandiana*, 59 (1941), 217–71.

Grosjean, P., 'La mort de S. Grégoire révelée à S. Colmán de Lann Elo', *Analecta Bollandiana* 76 (1958), 411–13.

Gwynn, A. & R.N. Hadcock, *Medieval religious houses, Ireland* (London, 1970).

Hammer, M., *The chronicle of Ireland (collected in the yeare 1571)* (Dublin, 1633; repr. Dublin, 1809).

Harbison, P., *The high crosses of Ireland*, 3 vols (Bonn & Dublin, 1992).

Hardiman, J. (ed.), *A chorographical description of West or h-Iar Connaught, written AD 1684 by Roderic O'Flaherty Esq.* (Irish Archaeological Society; Dublin, 1846; repr. Galway, 1978).

Herbert, M., 'An infancy narrative of Saint Ciarán', *Proceedings of the Harvard Celtic Colloquium*, 14 (1994), 1–8.

Herbert, M., 'Literary sea-voyages and early Munster hagiography' in R. Black, W. Gillies & R. Ó Maolalaigh (eds), *Celtic connections: Proceedings of the Tenth International Congress of Celtic Studies* (East Linton, 1999), 182–9.

Herity, M. (ed.), *Ordnance Survey letters, Laois* (Dublin, 2008).

Hogan, E., *Onomasticon goedelicum locorum et tribuum Hiberniae et Scotiae: an index, with identifications, to the Gaelic names of places and tribes* (Dublin & London, 1910).

Hull, V., 'Apgitir Chrábaid: the Alphabet of Piety', *Celtica*, 8 (1968), 44–89.

Hyde, D., 'The adventures of Léithin', *Celtic Review,* 10 (1915), 116–43.

Joynt, M. (ed.), *Tromdámh Guaire* (Medieval and Modern Series 2; Dublin, 1931).

Kehnel, A., 'The lands of St Ciarán' in H.A. King (ed.), *Clonmacnoise Studies*, 1 (1994), 11–17.

Kehnel, A., *Clonmacnois – the church and lands of St Ciarán: change and continuity in an Irish monastic foundation (6th to 16th century)* (Münster, 1997).

Kelleher, J.V., 'The Táin and the annals', *Ériu* 22 (1971), 107–27.

Kelly, F., *A guide to early Irish law* (Early Irish Law Series iii; Dublin, 1988).

Kelly, F., *Early Irish farming* (Early Irish Law Series iv; Dublin, 1997).

Kenney, J.F., *The sources for the early history of Ireland (ecclesiastical)* (New York, 1929; repr. Dublin, 1979).

Knott, E., 'A poem of prophecies', *Ériu*, 18 (1958), 55–84.

Lyons, J., 'Notes and queries: Raithlenn', *Journal of the Cork Historical and Archaeological Society*, 2 (1896), 449–51.

Mac Airt, S. (ed.), *Leabhar Branach: the Book of the O'Byrnes* (Dublin, 1944).

Mac Airt, S. (ed.), *The Annals of Inisfallen (MS Rawlinson B.503)* (Dublin, 1951).

Macalister, R.A.S. (ed.), 'The Life of Saint Finan', *Zeitschrift für celtische Philologie*, 2 (1899), 545–65.

Macalister, R.A.S., *The Latin and Irish Lives of Ciaran* (Translations of Christian Literature. Series V, Lives of the Celtic Saints; London & New York, 1921).

MacDonald, A., 'The "Cathedral", Temple Kelly and Temple Ciarán: notes from the annals', in H.A. King (ed.), *Clonmacnoise Studies*, 2 (2003), 125–35.

MacErlean, J., 'Synod of Ráith Breasail: boundaries of the dioceses of Ireland', *Archivium Hibernicum*, 3 (1914), 1–33.

McKay, P., *Placenames of Northern Ireland*, iv (Belfast, 1995).

Mac Shamhráin, A.S., 'The unity of Cóemgen and Ciarán', in K. Hannigan & W. Nolan (eds), *Wicklow: history and society* (Dublin, 1994), 139–50.

Mac Shamhráin, A.S., 'Fínán Camm', in J. Maguire & J. Quinn (eds), *Dictionary of Irish biography*, 9 vols (Dublin & Cambridge, 2009), iii, 779.

Meyer, K., 'Irish quatrains', *Zeitschrift für celtische Philologie*, 1(1897), 455–7.

Meyer, K., Cáin Adamnáin. An Old-Irish treatise on the Law of Adamnan (Anecdota Oxoniensia; Oxford, 1905).

Meyer, K., 'Wunderbare Geschichten von Corpre Cromm mac Feradaig', in idem, 'Neue Mitteilungen aus irischen Handschriften', *Archiv für celtische Lexikographie* 3:3 (1906), 224–6.

Meyer, K., *The triads of Ireland* (Royal Irish Academy Todd Lecture Series 13; Dublin, 1906).

Meyer, K., 'The Laud genealogies and tribal histories', *Zeitschrift für celtische Philologie* 8/9 (1911), 291–338.

Meyer, K., 'Mitteilungen aus irischen Handschriften', *Zeitschrift für celtische Philologie*, 12 (1918), 290–7.

Meyer, K., 'Mitteilungen aus irischen Handschriften', *Zeitschrift für celtische Philologie* 13 (1920), 3–30.

Mordek, H., 'Von Patrick zu Bonifatius ... Alkuin, Ferrières und die irischen Heiligen in einem westfränkischen Reliquienverzeichnis' in K. Herbers, H.H. Kortüm & C. Servatius (eds), *Ex Ipsis Rerum Documentis: Beiträge zur Mediävistik* (Sigmaringen, 1991), 55–68.

Mulcahy, D.B., *Beatha Naoimh Chiaráin Saighre: Life of S. Kieran (the Elder) of Seir* (Dublin, 1895).

Mulchrone, K. (ed.), *Bethu Phátraic. The tripartite Life of Patrick* (Dublin and London, 1939).

Murphy, D., *The Annals of Clonmacnoise being Annals of Ireland from the earliest period to AD 1408* (Royal Society of Antiquaries, extra vol., 1893–5; Dublin, 1896).

Murray, K., 'The dating of Branwen: the "Irish question" revisited' in J. Carey, K. Murray & C. Ó Dochartaigh (eds), *Sacred histories: a festschrift for Máire Herbert* (Dublin, 2015), 247–50.

Ní Dhonnchadha, M., 'The beginnings of Irish vernacular literary tradition' in *L'irlanda e gli irlandesi nell'alto medioevo* (*Settimane di studio della Fondazione Centro italiano di studi sull'alto Medioevo* 57) (Spoleto, 2010), 533–96.

Ní Ghrádaigh, J., '"But what exactly did she give?": Derbforgaill and the Nuns' Church at Clonmacnoise' in H.A. King (ed.), *Clonmacnoise Studies*, 2 (2003), 175–207.

O'Brien, C., *Stories from a sacred landscape: Croghan Hill to Clonmacnoise* (Tullamore, 2006).

O'Brien, C. & P.D. Sweetman, *Archaeological inventory of County Offaly* (Dublin, 1997).

O'Brien, M.A., *Corpus genealogiarum Hiberniae*, 1 (Dublin, 1962).

Ó Corráin, D., 'Studies in West Munster history: II. Alltraighe', *Journal of the Kerry Archaeological and Historical Society*, 2 (1969), 27–37.

O'Donovan, J., *Miscellany of the Celtic Society* (Dublin, 1849).

O'Donovan, J., *The antiquities of the County of Kerry* (Cork, 1983).

Ó Floinn, R., 'Clonmacnoise: art and patronage in the early medieval period' in H.A. King (ed.), *Clonmacnoise Studies*, 1 (1994), 87–100.

O'Grady, S.H., 'Betha Chiaráin tSaighre' in idem (ed.), *Silva Gadelica: a collection of tales in Irish*, 2 vols (London & Edinburgh, 1892), i, 1–16.

O'Hanlon, J., *The Lives of the Irish saints*, 10 vols (Dublin, 1875–1903).

Ó hAodha, D. (ed.), *Bethu Brigte* (Dublin, 1978).

O'Keeffe, J.G., 'The kings buried in Clonmacnois' in J. Fraser et al. (eds), *Irish texts*, 4 (London, 1934), 44–6.

O'Kelleher, A. & G. Schoepperle (eds), *Betha Colaim Chille: Life of Columcille* (Irish Foundation Series 1; Chicago, 1918).

Ó Lochlainn, C., 'Roadways in ancient Ireland' in J. Ryan (ed.), *Féil-sgríbhinn Eóin Mhic Néill: essays and studies presented to Professor Eoin MacNeill D.Litt. on the occasion of his seventieth birthday* (Dublin, 1940), 465–74.

Ó Muirgheasa, É., 'The holy wells of Donegal', *Béaloideas*, 6 (1936), 143–62.

Ó Muraíle, N., *Leabhar mór na ngenealach: The great book of Irish genealogies compiled (1645–66) by Dubhaltach Mac Fhirbhisigh* (Dublin, 2003).

Ó Murchadha, D., *Family names of County Cork* (Dún Laoghaire, 1985).

O'Rahilly, C. (ed.), *Five seventeenth-century political poems* (Dublin, 1952).

O'Rahilly, T.F., *Early Irish history and mythology* (Dublin, 1946).

Ó Riain, P., 'Boundary association in early Irish society', *Studia Celtica*, 7 (1972), 12–29.

Ó Riain, P., 'The saints of Cardiganshire' in J.L. Davies & D.P. Kirby (eds), *Cardiganshire County History*, 1 (Cardiff, 1994), 378–96.

Ó Riain, P., '*Codex Salmanticensis*: a provenance *inter Anglos* or *inter Hibernos?*' in T. Barnard, D. Ó Cróinín & K. Simms (eds), *A miracle of learning: essays in honour of William O'Sullivan* (Aldershot, 1997), 91–100.

Ó Riain, P., *The making of a saint: Finbarr of Cork, 600–1200* (Irish Texts Society, Subsidiary Series 5; London, 1997).

Ó Riain, P., *Feastdays of the saints: a history of Irish martyrologies* (Subsidia Hagiographica 86; Brussels, 2006).

Ó Riain, P., 'The Lives of Saint Ciarán, patron of the diocese of Ossory', *Ossory, Laois and Leinster*, 3 (2008), 25–42.

Ó Riain, P., 'Fíonán of Iveragh' in J. Crowley & J. Sheehan (eds), *The Iveragh peninsula: a cultural atlas of the Ring of Kerry* (Cork, 2009), 126–8.

Ó Riain, P., 'The O'Donohue Lives of the Salamancan Codex: the earliest collection of Irish saints' Lives?' in S. Sheehan, J. Findon & W. Follett (eds), *Gablánach in Scélaigecht: Celtic studies in honour of Ann Dooley* (Dublin, 2013), 38–52.

Ó Riain, P., *Four Tipperary saints: the Lives of Colum of Terryglass, Crónán of Roscrea, Mochaomhóg of Leigh and Ruadhán of Lorrha* (Dublin, 2014).

Ó Riain-Raedel, D., 'German influence on Munster church and kings in the twelfth century' in A. Smyth (ed.), *Seanchas: Studies in early and medieval Irish archaeology, history and literature in honour of Francis J. Byrne* (Dublin, 2000), 323–30.

Orme, N., *The saints of Cornwall* (Oxford, 2000).

Otway, C., 'A day at Clonmacnoise', *The Christian Examiner and Church of Ireland Magazine for 1832*, n.s. 1, 812–23, 875–96.

Otway, C., *A tour in Connaught comprising sketches of Clonmacnoise, Joyce Country, and Achill* (Dublin, 1839).

Pender, S. (ed.), 'The O Clery book of genealogies', *Analecta Hibernica*, 18 (1951), i–xxxiii, 1–198.

Plummer, C. (ed.), *Vitae sanctorum Hiberniae*, 2 vols (Oxford, 1910; repr. 1968).

Plummer, C. (ed.), *Bethada náem nÉrenn. Lives of Irish saints*, 2 vols (Oxford, 1922).

Plummer, C. (ed.), *Irish litanies* (Henry Bradshaw Society 62; London, 1925).

Plummer, C., *Miscellanea hagiographica Hibernica* (Subsidia Hagiographica 15; Brussels, 1925).

Radner, J., *Fragmentary annals of Ireland* (Dublin, 1978).

Reeves, W., *Ecclesiastical antiquities of Down, Connor and Dromore, consisting of a taxation of those dioceses, compiled in the Year MCCVI* (Dublin, 1847).

Rekdal, J.E., 'Memorials and cultural memory in Irish tradition' in J.E. Rekdal & E. Poppe (eds), *Medieval Irish perspectives on cultural memory* (Münster, 2014), 109–33.

Ryan, J., 'The abbatial succession at Clonmacnoise', in idem (ed.), *Féil-sgríbhinn Eóin Mhic Néill: essays and studies presented to Professor Eoin MacNeill D.Litt. on the occasion of his seventieth birthday* (Dublin, 1940), 490–507.

Ryan, J., *Clonmacnois: a historical summary* (Dublin, 1973).

Schneiders, M., 'The Irish calendar in the Karlsruhe Bede', *Archiv für Liturgiewissenschaft*, 31 (1989), 33–78.

Seabhac, An, *Uí Ráthach* (Baile Átha Cliath, n.d.).

Sharpe, R., 'Latin and Irish words for "book-satchel"', *Peritia*, 4 (1985), 152–6.

Sharpe, R., 'Quattuor sanctissimi episcopi: Irish saints before St Patrick' in D. Ó Corráin, L. Breatnach & K. McCone (eds), *Sages, saints and storytellers: Celtic studies in honour of Professor James Carney* (Maynooth, 1989), 376–99.

Sharpe, R., *Medieval Irish saints' Lives. An introduction to Vitae sanctorum Hiberniae* (Oxford, 1991).

Sperber, I., 'The Life of St Ciarán of Saigir' in W. Nolan & T.P. O'Neill (eds), *Offaly: history and society; interdisciplinary essays on the history of an Irish county* (Dublin, 1998), 131–52.

Stokes, W. (ed.), *Lives of the saints from the Book of Lismore* (Anecdota Oxoniensa; Oxford, 1890).

Stokes, W. (ed.), *The tripartite Life of St Patrick with other documents relating to that saint*, 2 vols (Rolls Series 89; London, 1887).

Stokes, W. (ed.), 'The Annals of Tigernach', *Revue Celtique*, 16 (1895), 374–419; 17 (1896), 6–33, 119–263, 337–420; 18 (1897), 9–59, 150–97, 267–303; rep. 2 vols, Felinfach, 1993).

Stokes, W., 'Cuimmín's poem on the saints of Ireland', *Zeitschrift für celtische Philologie*, 1 (1897), 59–73.

Swift, C., 'Sculptors and their customers: a study of Clonmacnoise grave-slabs' in H.A. King (ed.), *Clonmacnoise Studies*, 2 (2003), 105–23.

Tommasini, A., *Irish saints in Italy* (London, 1937).

Walsh, P. (ed.), *Genealogiae regum et sanctorum Hiberniae by the Four Masters* (Maynooth & Dublin, 1918).

Walsh, P., *The placenames of Westmeath* (Dublin, 1957).

Watson, W.J., *The history of the Celtic placenames of Scotland* (Edinburgh & London, 1926; repr. Dublin, 1986).

Williams, B., *The Annals of Ireland by Friar John Clyn* (Dublin, 2007).

Index of persons, places and peoples

Index of subjects

kite, *see* bird(s)
knife 15

lameness 62
lamp, lights miraculously 44
laymen 60, 82; former 46, 107
Leabhar na hUidhre, see Book of the Dun
    Cow
Leath Éireann / Half of Ireland 19
Lent 46
lion 24
litany 29
liturgy, xiv, 97
Lives, of saints xiii

manuscripts: **Brussels**, Bibliothèque
    Royale 4190–200, 10; 7672–4
    (*Salmanticensis*) xiv, 12, 55, 57;
    Dublin, Marsh's Library, Z.3.1.5
    (formerly V.3.4) 10, 12, 32; **Gotha**
    I.81 32, 34, 100
maoir 55
marsh 84
martyrologies: xiii–iv; Hieronymian xiii,
    4; of Gorman 75; of Óengus 90, 93–
    4, 96, 99, 112, 116; of Tallaght 51;
    Roman xiv
mass 82
meat 49, 62, 107
medical doctors 87
merchants, from Gaul 26
milk 17, 48, 58, 67, 87, 108
millstone 16
miracles, posthumous 115
monster, terrifying 53
moon, silver xvi
mulberries 41
music, sleep-inducing 41
mysteries, divine 21

nakedness 20
numbers: **3** 40, 48, 83, 85, 87–8; **5** 85, 88,
    95; **7** 40, 45, 81, 85–6; **8** 42; **9** 42,
    82; **12** 39, 42; **20** 31, 36, 41, 44; **27**
    39, 43; **30** 31–2, 35–6, 49, 85; **33** 98,

107; **55** 53; **200** 85, 91; **300** 49, 83,
    99; **350** 108; **5,000** 85

oak, carriage of 58
oath, swearing of 68
obedience 62, 66, 85, 97, 112
octave 51
O'Donohue, Lives 55
officials, of church 8
onion (s) 88, 121
ox(en) 16, 43, 64

paganism 49
paralytics 84, 88
parish / *paruchia* 27, 36, 41
petitions / requests, three 48, 73, 108, 115
pigs 39, 41, 82
pilgrim(age) 23, 30, 44–5, 46, 65
pincers, of smith 88
plague 73
plough(ing) 16, 43
Polaire Chiaráin 91
preaching 71, 107
pregnancy, termination of 38, 102
pre-Patrician, saints 28, 37, 99–101
prior, of monastery 21, 39
prophet / prophecy 24, 29, 41, 56, 81, 90,
    94, 97, 114
psalms / psalmist 14–15, 18, 72
psalter, copied 71; of Cashel xv

quern 18

rain, spares saint 86–7
Registry, of Clonmacnoise 9
Relic(s) 4, 8, 99; *adhart Chiaráin* (stone
    pillow) 6, 26, 98; altar 4; bell 4;
    crozier 4, 53; *Matha Mór* (gospel-
    book?) 4; *odhar Chiaráin* (hide of
    Ciarán's dun cow) 6, 18; *Óireanach*
    (Ciarán's crozier) 4; rib 76
ring, gold 22
rites, last 66
rivers, in flood 61, 68
rock(s), angels on / cross on 72, 91